Stevenson College Edinburgh.
Library

A25242

KT-583-976

Racial Discrimination

ISSUES

Volume 115

Series Editor

Craig Donnellan

Assistant Editor

Lisa Firth

STEVENSON COLLEGE
LIBRARY

ACC. N̲ **WITHDRAWN** A25242

CLASS/LOC 305.8

CAT 31|06 Aew | PROC NS-2-2-06

Independence

Educational Publishers
Cambridge

WITHDRAWN
Stevenson College Edinburgh
Bankhead Ave, EDIN EH11 4DE

First published by Independence
PO Box 295
Cambridge CB1 3XP
England

© Craig Donnellan 2006

Copyright
This book is sold subject to the condition that it shall not,
by way of trade or otherwise, be lent, resold, hired out or otherwise
circulated in any form of binding or cover other than that in which it
is published without the publisher's prior consent.

Photocopy licence
The material in this book is protected by copyright. However, the
purchaser is free to make multiple copies of particular articles for instructional
purposes for immediate use within the purchasing institution.
Making copies of the entire book is not permitted.

British Library Cataloguing in Publication Data
Racial Discrimination – (Issues Series)
I. Donnellan, Craig II. Series
305.8

ISBN 1 86168 348 0

Printed in Great Britain
MWL Print Group Ltd

Layout by
Lisa Firth

Cover
The illustration on the front cover is by
Simon Kneebone.

CONTENTS

Introduction

Racial Discrimination is the one hundred and fifteenth volume in the **Issues** series. The aim of this series is to offer up-to-date information about important issues in our world.

Racial Discrimination looks at general issues relating to race and racism, as well as the relationship between race, religion and national identity.

The information comes from a wide variety of sources and includes:
Government reports and statistics
Newspaper reports and features
Magazine articles and surveys
Website material
Literature from lobby groups
and charitable organisations.

It is hoped that, as you read about the many aspects of the issues explored in this book, you will critically evaluate the information presented. It is important that you decide whether you are being presented with facts or opinions. Does the writer give a biased or an unbiased report? If an opinion is being expressed, do you agree with the writer?

Racial Discrimination offers a useful starting-point for those who need convenient access to information about the many issues involved. However, it is only a starting-point. At the back of the book is a list of organisations which you may want to contact for further information.

*****

Racism

Information taken from a ChildLine Information Sheet

'I want to move house. I'm mixed race and a gang of girls keep punching me and taking my money. Mum has contacted the council but nothing's happened.'
Sylvia, 12

Racism is treating someone differently or unfairly simply because they belong to a different race or culture. People can also experience prejudice because of their religion or nationality.

One person can act in a racist way or a group of people or a whole community of people can be racist.

Racism can be expressed in many different ways. These can include:

- being called names
- being teased, insulted or threatened
- being hit, pulled, pinched or kicked
- having your bag, mobile phone or other possessions taken
- being ignored or left out
- being forced to do things you don't want to do
- having your things or home damaged.

Racism can have a terrible effect. Children and young people can become lonely, isolated, angry and depressed. They may lose self-confidence and become terrified of going to school or going out alone. To avoid racism, they may keep away from situations where racist behaviour occurs and pretend to be ill, play truant from school, or be scared to leave their house.

How does ChildLine help?

'ChildLine is great. You can talk about what you want and it's just between you and them.'
John, 13

Each year ChildLine receives over 500 calls and letters from children about racist bullying, and about 50 calls and letters from children who experienced other forms of racism.

ChildLine takes children's and young people's problems seriously, giving them a chance to talk in confidence about their concerns or worries, however large or small.

Children and young people are given direct help, advice and support on the helpline. In some situations, the ChildLine counsellor can put a young person in touch with social services, the police, or some other place where they can receive help.

ChildLine has a policy of confidentiality. ChildLine counsellors will not pass on any information about a caller to anyone else and all conversations are private. ChildLine will only break confidentiality if the young person or someone else they talk about is in a life-threatening situation.

Children and young people trust ChildLine, as it is anonymous and confidential. Being able to speak in confidence about serious problems such as racism, bullying or abuse may also help to prevent young people doing something that will cause them pain or harm.

ChildLine is free and available 24 hours a day, seven days a week.

Why are people racist?

'I'm the only Asian person in my class and used to get picked on for my colour, but I dealt with it. I feel now though that it's made me racist against white people. I hate myself for it. I just wish people from different races would leave each other alone.'
Shireen, 15

Unfortunately racism exists in all races and cultures. Racists can feel threatened by anyone who is from a different race or culture, or they may just be intolerant and pick on anyone who is different from them.

We are not born racist. Our views and beliefs develop as we grow up. If a child or young person grows up within a racist family, or has friends who are racist, they may believe that racism is normal and acceptable.

WE'RE ALL THE SAME?!! HA! HA!!

... EXCEPT I'M THE ONE TRYING NOT TO BE RACIST...

Prejudice of any kind is often based on ignorance and fear of anything unfamiliar.

Challenging racism

'They bully me because of my colour. They call me racist names, hit me and make comments about my family. The hitting hurts, but the words hurt more. My dad has suggested that I punch the bullies. I think this will make things worse though, as the bullies are very popular. The whole school could end up hating me.'
Nat, 12

Racism is against the law and should not be accepted under any circumstances. The Government has put anti-racist laws into place to protect all members of the community. In many schools young people and teachers work together to produce anti-bullying policies, which include sections on racist bullying.

I'm being bullied. What should I do?

'We recently moved from Liverpool to Glasgow and I keep being picked on because of my accent. They swear at me and push my head down the toilet. I've told my parents and the teachers, but they've done nothing to help.'
Chris, 14

You should not feel ashamed. It's not your fault, but it is important you get help. No one deserves racism.

You should find someone to talk to – maybe a friend or someone at your school, like a teacher. They may be able to tell you what you can do about it or help you decide what to do next. Try and keep yourself safe. For instance, you could walk home with someone you know rather than on your own.

What does the law say about racism?

Racist incidents, ranging from harassment and abuse to physical violence, are against the law.

Encouraging others to be racist – known as 'inciting racial hatred' – is also a criminal offence.

Racist things in newspapers or on TV, radio or the internet break media codes of practice. If you believe you have seen anything racist – in an advert or a story or something similar – you can make a complaint to the Press Complaints Commission at www.pcc.org.uk or the Office of Communications at the website www.ofcom.org.uk

The Race Relations (Amendment) Act 2000 made it illegal to discriminate against a person at work, in education and housing. It is also against the law to treat anyone differently because of their colour when providing goods and services, like shopping and home repairs. The Race Relations Order 1997, which applies to Northern Ireland, covers the same issues.

How can racism be stopped?

'I get really annoyed that lots of people at my school are racist towards Asians. I'm not Asian, but have friends who are. My family doesn't like Asian people.'
Mandy, 14

If you see racism, report it. Don't ignore what happens. Let the person suffering racism know that you've seen what's going on and let them know you are concerned.

Encourage the person experiencing racism to tell someone.

If someone does believe they have suffered racism, they have the right to bring their complaint before an employment tribunal or a court.

Further information and advice

Britkid
This is a website about race, racism and life – as seen through the eyes of the Britkids.
Website: www.britkid.org

Commission for Racial Equality
A government organisation that aims to protect all UK citizens from racism.
St Dunstan's House
201-211 Borough High Street
London SE1 1GZ
Tel: 020 7939 0000
Email: info@cre.gov.uk
Website: www.cre.gov.uk

Equal Opportunities Commission
A government organisation that aims to protect UK citizens from all forms of discrimination, including racism and sexism.
Arndale House, Arndale Centre
Manchester M4 3EQ
Tel: 0845 601 5901
Website: www.eoc.org.uk

Equality Commission Northern Ireland
Andras House
60 Great Victoria Street
Belfast BT2 7BB
Tel: 02890 500600
Website: www.equalityni.org

■ Information from ChildLine, March 2004. For more information, visit www.childline.org.uk or see page 41 for their address details.
© ChildLine

Children and ethnicity

Children under 16 by ethnic group, 2001-02 [1]

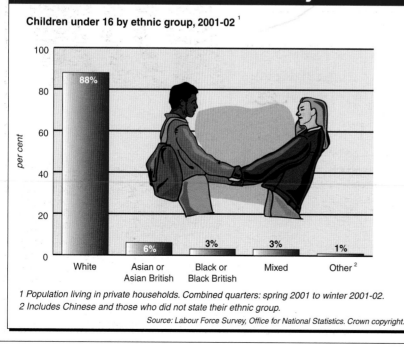

	per cent
White	88%
Asian or Asian British	6%
Black or Black British	3%
Mixed	3%
Other [2]	1%

1 Population living in private households. Combined quarters: spring 2001 to winter 2001-02.
2 Includes Chinese and those who did not state their ethnic group.
Source: Labour Force Survey, Office for National Statistics. Crown copyright.

Population size

7.9% from a non-White ethnic group

The majority of the UK population in 2001 were White (92 per cent). The remaining 4.6 million (or 7.9 per cent) people belonged to other ethnic groups.

Indians were the largest of these groups, followed by Pakistanis, those of Mixed ethnic backgrounds, Black Caribbeans, Black Africans and Bangladeshis. The remaining minority ethnic groups each accounted for less than 0.5 per cent of the UK population and together accounted for a further 1.4 per cent.

Around half of the non-White population were Asians of Indian, Pakistani, Bangladeshi or other Asian origin. A further quarter were Black, that is Black Caribbean, Black African or Other Black. Fifteen per cent of the non-White population were from the Mixed ethnic group. About a third of this group were from White and Black Caribbean backgrounds.

There were almost 691,000 White Irish people in Great Britain accounting for 1 per cent of the GB population.

In Great Britain the number of people who came from an ethnic group other than White grew by 53 per cent between 1991 and 2001, from 3.0 million in 1991 to 4.6 million in 2001. In 1991 ethnic group data were not collected on the Northern Ireland Census.

Sources

- Census, April 1991 and 2001, Office for National Statistics;
- Census, April 2001, General Register Office for Scotland;
- Census, April 2001, Northern Ireland Statistics and Research Agency.

Notes

Census ethnic group questions: In both 1991 and 2001 respondents were asked to which ethnic group they considered themselves to belong. The question asked in 2001 was more extensive than that asked in 1991, so that people could tick 'Mixed' for the first time. This change in answer categories may account for a small part of the observed increase in the minority ethnic population over the period. Different versions of the ethnic group question were asked in England and Wales, in Scotland and in Northern Ireland, to reflect local differences in the requirement for information. However, results are comparable across the UK as a whole.

Non-White ethnic group includes all minority ethnic groups but not White Irish or Other White groups.

- Information reprinted with kind permission from the Office for National Statistics – for more information please visit their website at www.statistics.gov.uk

© Crown copyright

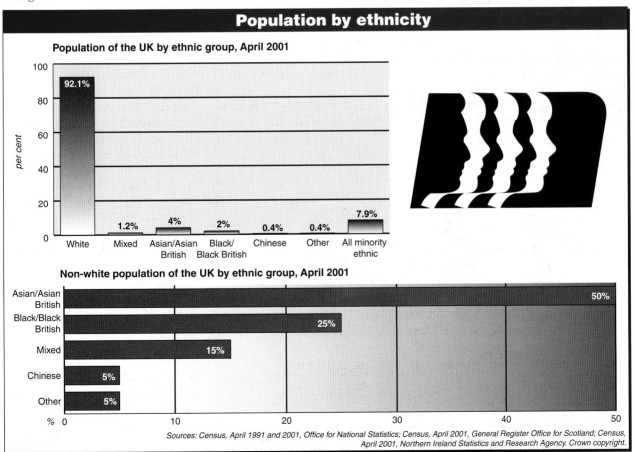

Population by ethnicity

Population of the UK by ethnic group, April 2001

per cent

- White: 92.1%
- Mixed: 1.2%
- Asian/Asian British: 4%
- Black/Black British: 2%
- Chinese: 0.4%
- Other: 0.4%
- All minority ethnic: 7.9%

Non-white population of the UK by ethnic group, April 2001

- Asian/Asian British: 50%
- Black/Black British: 25%
- Mixed: 15%
- Chinese: 5%
- Other: 5%

Sources: Census, April 1991 and 2001, Office for National Statistics; Census, April 2001, General Register Office for Scotland; Census, April 2001, Northern Ireland Statistics and Research Agency. Crown copyright.

Words

Some people worry a bit about which words are okay to use when they're talking about 'race'. Most people know words which are meant to be insulting, which are meant to put people down, but aren't so sure about other words.

Take someone who has a mother who is black and a father who is white. At one time they would have been called a 'half-caste' but this is now usually thought to be a bit insulting. 'Mixed race' was used next, but nowadays most people in this situation seem to prefer 'dual heritage'.

Remember the old playground rhyme:

'Sticks and stones may break my bones but names will never hurt me.'

This is not true – anyone who has been called names they don't like knows that. But how do we know which names and words will hurt? The best test is to ask, but this is not always easy or possible for everyone. To help with this, lots of people have been asked about this article to try to get it right.

The people who ought to decide whether a name or 'label' is okay (or not) are the people for whom the name is used, the people who have to wear the label.

The people who ought to decide whether a name or 'label' is okay (or not) are the people for whom the name is used, the people who have to wear the label

---

- If young people don't like being called 'kids' then adults should ask them what they want to be called.
- If someone who can't walk doesn't like being called a 'cripple' then others should respect that.
- The same goes for girls who don't like to be referred to as 'birds'.

Words which people generally think are okay

Black

People with roots in Africa or the Caribbean generally prefer this word to describe themselves (though some older people may not). Of course they are not really black like shoes can be black, but then 'white' people are not really white, are they? One of the reasons the word 'black' is preferred is that in the past people were often taught that black = bad or evil, and many people now want to say that there is nothing bad or evil about dark skin and that they are proud of it. As long ago as the 1960s black

Racism – what is it?

Information from Kick It Out

Racism

Racism is the belief that because people are a different colour, or from another country or part of the world, they are inferior. Most commonly racism is prejudice backed up by power.

Race

The word racism comes from this word. 'Race' was used by scientists in the 19th century to classify groups of people by the colour of their skin. Scientists have now proved that all of us, as human beings – black, white or brown – have the same ancestors.

Prejudice

Prejudice is judgement based upon ignorance, making up your mind about someone or some group before you really know them.

Discrimination

Discrimination is using prejudice to treat a person or group less well than you would normally. For example some people are prevented from getting a job because the employer dislikes the sound of their name, their skin colour, sex, disability or religion. In fact it is against the law to discriminate against someone for these reasons.

Racist attacks

If someone is attacked and feels they were targeted because of the colour of their skin this constitutes a racist attack.

- The above information is reprinted with kind permission from Kick It Out. Visit www.kickitout.org for more information or see page 41 for their address details.

© Kick It Out

people in the USA summed this up in the phrase 'black is beautiful'. Some people with Asian roots call themselves 'black' but most don't.

African-Caribbean
This is the term people with roots in the Caribbean tend to prefer, as an alternative to 'black'. They prefer it to what they used to be called, which was 'West Indian'.

Asian
This is the most general word for people with roots or family connections in India, Pakistan, Bangladesh and Sri Lanka. You aren't likely to annoy anyone by using it.

Pakistani, Indian, Bangladeshi, Chinese etc.
If you know someone has roots or family connections in one of these places then one of these words is fine, though people can be touchy if you kind of suggest they are not really British when they think they are. If you had a friend with an Italian name because her Italian grandparents moved to Britain in 1950, would you

How do we know which names and words will hurt? The best test is to ask, but this is not always easy or possible

call her Italian or British? Perhaps you would not be sure, perhaps it might depend on whether she felt a bit Italian herself, spoke Italian, went to an Italian-speaking Catholic church?

Roots or family connections in...
This is a useful expression. Taking India as an example, some people in Britain came here from India in the past few years (not many, actually); some people have been here forty years, others (almost everyone under the age of 25) were born here. In this mixture some have Indian passports, most have British passports and most know no home other than Britain. They are British, but they have roots or family connections in India.

Words which people don't like much

Coloured
An old-fashioned word which seems to want to avoid saying 'black'. White people are often more comfortable with it than, say, 'black . . .'

Immigrant
This simply means someone who has moved their home from one country to another. It is often disliked because most of Britain's black and Asian people are not immigrants, they were born here. British people who moved their homes from here to somewhere else (like Australia, America, India or Africa) were usually called 'settlers'. Funny that.

Paki, Chinky
Sometimes people use these words as a shortened form of the full word, as an abbreviation. Pakistanis and Chinese people hate it. More often, Paki is used on purpose as a general, insulting word for anyone with Pakistani, Indian or Bangladeshi roots, and then it's just as insulting as the range of other words which most people know (so there's no need to spell them out here).

Ethnic minorities
This is a funny phrase because it's often used in quite a vague way. Actually, you will find that people often use it when they mean black and Asian people, though ethnic has nothing to do with colour. The Irish in Britain are a minority ethnic group. You could say Welsh people are an ethnic group.

Muslim, Sikh, Hindu etc.
Sometimes a person's religion is more important to them than their family's roots, so it is sometimes better to describe them as a Sikh (for example) than as an Indian.

■ The above information is reprinted with kind permission from BritKid. Visit www.britkid.org or see page 41 for address details.

© BritKid

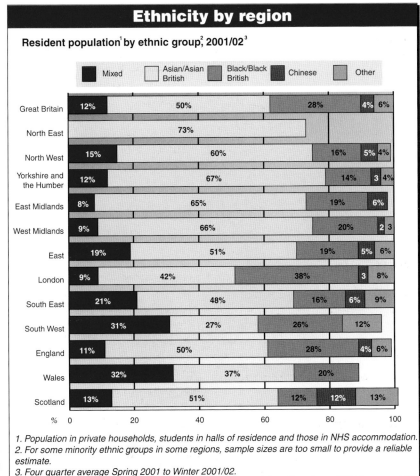

Ethnicity by region

Resident population[1] by ethnic group[2], 2001/02[3]

Legend: Mixed | Asian/Asian British | Black/Black British | Chinese | Other

Region	Mixed	Asian/Asian British	Black/Black British	Chinese	Other
Great Britain	12%	50%	28%	4%	6%
North East		73%			
North West	15%	60%	16%	5%	4%
Yorkshire and the Humber	12%	67%	14%	3	4%
East Midlands	8%	65%	19%		6%
West Midlands	9%	66%	20%	2	3
East	19%	51%	19%	5%	6%
London	9%	42%	38%	3	8%
South East	21%	48%	16%	6%	9%
South West	31%	27%	26%	12%	
England	11%	50%	28%	4%	6%
Wales	32%	37%	20%		
Scotland	13%	51%	12%	12%	13%

% 0   20   40   60   80   100

1. Population in private households, students in halls of residence and those in NHS accommodation.
2. For some minority ethnic groups in some regions, sample sizes are too small to provide a reliable estimate.
3. Four quarter average Spring 2001 to Winter 2001/02.
Source: Labour Force Survey, ONS. Crown copyright.

Word rage

CRE boss Trevor Phillips sparked a massive controversy last week when he asked: 'Is it really offensive to call someone "coloured"?'

By Dominic Bascombe

An almighty row has broken out after the head of the Commission for Racial Equality, Trevor Phillips, criticised a number of equality standards including whether the term 'coloured' was offensive.

Speaking at the Conservative Party Muslim Forum last week, Phillips returned to his recent theme of questioning the level of racial integration in Britain and spoke of a 'highway code' for integration.

'In Britain we have always been multi-ethnic – Scots, Welsh, Irish, Protestant, Catholic, and so on'

'In Britain we have always been multi-ethnic – Scots, Welsh, Irish, Protestant, Catholic, and so on. We have our hard laws that bind us all to parliamentary democracy, equality of men and women, the care of children, settling our disputes peacefully and so on.

Rules

'But we also have many unspoken rules, which are the equivalent of the "highway code" for our multi-ethnic society. We respect others' ways of worshipping. We compromise on dress codes – what we wear at work may not be what we wear at home. And above all we use the English language for everyday intercourse with others – even if there is only one person in the group who does not speak some other language,' he told forum delegates.

Phillips went on to question whether some attempts at integration were valid.

'Should councils print all their important documents in several languages to encourage participation, or is this encouraging separatism?' he asked.

'What should we do about holy days which are not bank holidays for example? Should we put off that important meeting because it's Yom Kippur, even though only one of the people attending is Jewish? Are judges right to say that school uniform may not be compulsory for the devout – even though for some it is compliant with Islamic modesty? Is it really offensive to call someone "coloured"? We need to find ways of reaching a national agreement on some of these issues,' the CRE bigwig said.

Since he raised these concerns his statements have caused a ruckus amongst black activists.

Lee Jasper, the Mayor of London's race adviser, said: 'Trevor Phillips has got his facts wrong. The census analysts at the Greater London Authority, and leading researchers nationally, have found that London and the rest of Britain are becoming less, not more, segregated. Any chair of the Commission for Racial Equality who does not know whether councils should print documents in several languages, or holy days like Yom Kippur should be respected, or whether "coloured" is an appropriate term, should consider whether he is in the right job.'

Perhaps the most contentious aspect of Phillips' statement is whether the term 'coloured' was offensive.
10 October 2005

■ The above information is reprinted with kind permission from the Voice. Visit www.voice-online.net for more information.
© Gleaner Voice Group

What is racial discrimination?

Information reprinted with permission from the Commission for Racial Equality

The Race Relations Act is concerned with people's actions and the effects of their actions, not their opinions or beliefs. Racial discrimination is not the same as racial prejudice. It is not necessary to prove that the other person intended to discriminate against you: you only have to show that you received less favourable treatment as a result of what they did.

Under the Race Relations Act, it is unlawful for a person to discriminate on racial grounds against another. The Act defines racial grounds as including race, colour, nationality or ethnic or national origins.

To bring a case under the Race Relations Act, you have to show you have been discriminated against in one or more ways that are unlawful under the Act.

There are four main types of racial discrimination: direct, indirect, victimisation and harassment. The following text describes each in turn.

Direct racial discrimination

This occurs when you are able to show that you have been treated less favourably on racial grounds than others in similar circumstances. To prove this, it will help if you can give an example of someone from a different racial group who, in similar circumstances, has been, or would have been treated more favourably than you. Racist abuse and harassment are forms of direct discrimination.

Indirect racial discrimination

Indirect racial discrimination may fall into one of two categories depending on the racial grounds of discrimination.

The first is on grounds of colour or nationality, under the original definition in the Race Relations Act.

COMMISSION FOR RACIAL EQUALITY

The second is on grounds of race, ethnic or national origin. This was introduced by the Race Relations Act (Amendment) Regulations 2003 to comply with the EC Race Directive.

On grounds of colour or nationality

This occurs when an apparently non-discriminatory requirement or condition which applies equally to everyone:

- can only be met by a considerably smaller proportion of people from a particular racial group; and
- which is to the detriment of a person from that group because he or she cannot meet it; and
- the requirement or condition cannot be justified on non-racial grounds.

For example, a rule that employees or pupils must not wear headgear could exclude Sikh men and boys who wear a turban, or Jewish men or boys who wear a yarmulka, in accordance with practice within their racial group.

On grounds of race, ethnic or national origin

This occurs when a provision, criterion or practice which, on the face of it, has nothing to do with race and is applied equally to everyone:

- puts or would put people of the same race or ethnic or national origins at a particular disadvantage when compared with others; and
- puts a person of that race or ethnic or national origin at that disadvantage; and
- cannot be shown to be a proportionate means of achieving a legitimate aim.

The definition of indirect discrimination on the grounds of race, ethnic or national origin is in general terms broader than on the grounds of colour or nationality and as a result it may be easier to establish racial discrimination than previously on that ground.

Victimisation

This has a special legal meaning under the Race Relations Act. It occurs if you are treated less favourably than others in the same circumstances because you have complained about racial discrimination, or supported someone else who has. A complaint of racial discrimination means that someone has:

NO HEADWEAR

- brought proceedings under the Race Relations Act against the discriminator or anyone else; or
- given evidence or information in connection with proceedings brought by another person under the Race Relations Act; or
- done anything under the Race Relations Act or with reference to it; or
- alleged that a person has acted in a way which would breach the Race Relations Act. The complaint does not need to expressly claim discrimination when making the complaint.

Harassment

The definition of harassment introduced by the Race Relations Act 1976 (Amendment) Regulations 2003 applies when the discrimination is on grounds of race or ethnic or national origins, but not colour or nationality. Harassment on grounds of colour or nationality amounts to less favourable treatment and may be unlawful direct discrimination.

A person harasses another on grounds of race or ethnic or national origins when he or she engages in unwanted conduct that has the purpose or effect of:
- violating that other person's dignity; or
- creating an intimidating or hostile, degrading, humiliating or offensive environment for them.

Harassment is unlawful not only in the context of employment, but also within:
- partnerships
- trade unions
- qualifying bodies
- vocational training; and
- employment agencies.

It is also an unlawful form of discrimination in education, planning, within public authorities, in the provision of goods, facilities, services and premises, and in relation to the training and employment of barristers and advocates.

- The above information is reprinted with kind permission from the Commission for Racial Equality. Visit www.cre.gov.uk for more information or see page 41 for details.
© Commission for Racial Equality

What is racial harassment?

Information from the Monitoring Group

Racial harassment covers a range of acts that breach both criminal and civil law. Although 'racial harassment' is not recognised by existing law, 'harassment' is a criminal offence, and is punishable in certain circumstances. In addition, 'incitement to racial hatred' is an offence under the Public Order Act, though this cannot at present be prosecuted without the consent of the Attorney General. Nowhere in law are the two aspects of racial harassment clearly brought together.

Racial harassment can occur in a number of ways. For example:
- Unprovoked assaults including common assault; actual bodily harm; and grievous bodily harm.
- Damage to property including breaking windows, doors and fences and within the perimeter of the house.
- The daubing of slogans and/or graffiti of slogans and/or graffiti of a racial nature within or in the proximity of the perimeter of the house concerned.
- The insertion of rags, paper, rubbish and/or any material which can be and/or has been set alight through openings, or within the perimeter of the property concerned.
- The insertion of excrement, eggs, paint, faeces, rubbish and/or other noxious and/or offensive substances through an opening in the house concerned or within its perimeter.
- The sending of threatening and/or abusive telephone calls of a racial nature.
- Verbal racial abuse.
- Repeated vandalism of a property belonging to the person concerned or any member of his/her household.
- Threatening and abusive behaviour including spitting.
- Participation in any activity which is calculated to deter the person from occupying a particular property.
- Attempted murder or murder.

What is the common definition used by the police or the local authority?

The Macpherson Inquiry into the death of Stephen Lawrence, better known as the Lawrence Report, recommended that the definition of a racist incident is as follows:

'A racist incident is any incident which is perceived to be racist by the victim or any other person' (p.328).

The Metropolitan Police and the London Borough of Ealing have now adopted this definition. This means that if you or another person tells a

police officer or the housing officer that you perceive an incident to be racist then they must investigate and record the incident as a racist incident.

Remember you should report all racist incidents as quickly as possible.

- The above information is reprinted with kind permission from the Monitoring Group. Please visit www.monitoring-group.co.uk for more information.

© The Monitoring Group

Police log 1,000 racist incidents a week

By John Steele

Racist incidents recorded by police, a category that will include the murder of Anthony Walker, are running at around 1,000 a week in England and Wales, according to Home Office figures.

In the last year for which statistics are available, 2003-04, there were 52,694 racist incidents recorded, a seven per cent rise from 49,078 in the previous year.

The highest figure was 54,370, in 2001-02, but recorded levels of racist incidents have been rising since 1996-97, when the total was 13,151.

The overall number of incidents recorded reflects the definition used since the 1999 Macpherson report into the murder of another black teenager, Stephen Lawrence.

It stated that a racist incident was one 'which is perceived to be racist by the victim or any other person'.

However, police do not record all incidents as offences. In 2003-04 there were 35,022 racially or religiously aggravated offences recorded. This had risen from 31,034 in the previous year.

Racially aggravated murders were rare. Of the total of racist incidents last year around half were classed as harassment.

The racially aggravated category will also include offences of violence. One-third of racially or religiously aggravated offences were cleared up by police.

Of the 5,692 defendants prosecuted for such offences in 2003, 2,440 were convicted in magistrates' courts and 457 for more serious offences in Crown courts. There were 681 cautions.

Greater encouragement by police to report racist incidents, and a greater willingness to record and investigate cases, have contributed to the rising numbers. The adoption of the Macpherson definition led to a sharp rise.

However, it is also argued that racist offences have been rising in real terms and are still under-reported.

3 August 2005

© Telegraph Group Limited 2005

Schools under fire as child race crimes rocket 74%

By Michael Howie

The number of children charged with race crimes in Scotland has soared by 74 per cent in the past three years.

Some 197 youngsters were referred to the Children's Reporter for race-related offences in 2004-5 compared to 113 in 2002-3. The figures, released by the Scottish Executive in a written parliamentary answer, have sparked accusations that schools are not doing enough to tackle racism in the playground.

Last night (7 September 2005), anti-racism campaign-ers called on teachers to take 'proactive' measures to stamp out racism in schools.

Morag Patrick, a senior officer with the Commission for Racial Equality Scotland, said: 'The increase in the number of children reported for racist crimes is concerning. They clearly indicate that racism remains a problem.

'They also reinforce recent CRE research in which ethnic minority participants expressed anxiety about the effect on their children of racist abuse in schools and said that schools were not doing enough to tackle the issue.'

Bill McGregor, the general secretary of the Headteachers' Association of Scotland, said he recognised that racism among children was 'a problem', but insisted that 'the great majority of schools, if not all, are working hard to do something about it.'

He also suggested the rise could partly be explained by an increased willingness to report crimes of racism.

The Scottish National Party's social justice spokeswoman, Christine Grahame, said: 'In just three years, we have seen the number of children accused of racial offences almost double. That indicates a very serious problem, not just for the victims of such offences but also for the wider communities in which these children live.'

8 September 2005

© The Scotsman

Victims of crime

Highest risk for Mixed race people

In 2002/03, adults from a Mixed race or Asian background were more likely than those from other ethnic groups to be victims of crime in England and Wales. Almost half (46 per cent) of adults of Mixed race had been the victim of a crime in the previous 12 months. This compared with 30 per cent of Asians. Black adults and those from the 'Chinese or other' group experienced similar levels of crime to White people.

Young adults are more likely than older people to be victims of crime and minority ethnic groups have a younger age structure than the White ethnic group. After allowing for their younger age structure, Asian adults were no more likely than those from other groups to be victims of crime. In contrast, Mixed race people still had higher risks of crime after allowing for age and the type of area in which they lived.

When overall crime is split between personal crime and household crime, adults from Mixed race backgrounds still had the highest risk of both types of crime. Seventeen per cent of Mixed race people had been the victim of a personal crime (common assault, robbery, theft from the person and other personal theft) compared with between 7 and 9 per cent of people from other ethnic groups. A third (34 per cent) of Mixed race people had experienced household crime (which includes

Almost half (46 per cent) of adults of Mixed race had been the victim of a crime in the previous 12 months

vehicle theft, vandalism and burglary) compared with between 18 and 23 per cent of people from other ethnic groups.

In 2002/03 one in ten Mixed race households (10 per cent) had experienced a burglary in the previous 12 months compared with less than 1 in 20 of other households (between 3 and 4 per cent).

People from Mixed race backgrounds were also at greater risk than other ethnic groups of violence. Eleven per cent reported being the victim of a violent crime in the previous 12 months, compared with no more than 5 per cent in any other ethnic group.

In 2002/03, the risk of being the victim of a racially motivated incident was higher for members of minority ethnic groups than for White people. Four per cent of Mixed race people, 3 per cent of Asians, 2 per cent of Black people, and 2 per cent of those from a 'Chinese or other' background had experienced a crime they thought was racially motivated

in the previous 12 months. This compared with less than 1 per cent of White people.

People from minority ethnic groups were much more likely than White people to report that they were 'very worried' about crime. For instance, 43 per cent of Asian people were very worried about violent crime compared with 19 per cent of White people. Levels of worry about crime are higher in inner-city areas and for those who have experienced crime. Even after allowing for these factors, people from minority ethnic groups were still more likely than White people to be worried about crime.

Source
British Crime Survey, 2002/2003, Home Office

Notes
All BCS crime includes: all personal crime and all household crime.

All personal crime includes: assault; robbery; theft from the person; and other personal theft.

All household crime includes: bicycle theft; burglary; theft in a dwelling; other household theft, thefts of/from vehicles, and vandalism to household property/vehicles.

Racially motivated crime: British Crime Survey respondents are asked, in respect of all crimes of which they were victims, whether they thought the incident was racially motivated. Victims are defined as anyone who judged that racial motivation was present in any household or personal crime which they had experienced in the relevant year, including threats.

Violent crime: levels of worry about violent crime were calculated using four types of violence: mugging/robbery, rape, physical attack by a stranger and racially motivated assault.
Published 21 March 2005

■ Information from the Office for National Statistics.

© *Crown copyright*

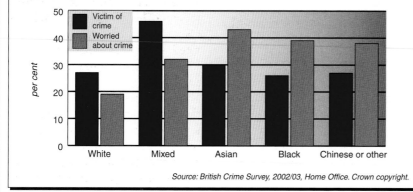

Victims of crime

Proportion of adults who have experienced a crime within the last 12 months, and proportion of adults who felt very worried about violent crime: by ethnic group, 2002/03, England and Wales

per cent — Victim of crime / Worried about crime — White, Mixed, Asian, Black, Chinese or other

Source: British Crime Survey, 2002/03, Home Office. Crown copyright.

Racism at work

A crime in anyone's language

Racism at work can be direct or subtle, conscious or unwitting.

It can come from your boss, from the people you work with, or be built into the way your organisation works.

Racist behaviour can be against the law, and this article explains your rights if you think you have been a victim of racial discrimination.

Direct discrimination occurs when a worker is treated less favourably on the grounds of race, colour, nationality, ethnic or national origin

It takes a positive commitment from the whole organisation – managers and staff. When employers and unions work together it can make a real difference.

Racism at work

Racism occurs when you are treated differently to your colleagues because of your race or ethnic origin.

Common examples are when someone is:

- called names
- overlooked for promotion
- denied training
- denied overtime and other benefits
- only offered unpopular shifts
- shouted at
- bullied
- selected for redundancy
- denied holiday entitlement.

Racism is bad for workers… and employees.

You can suffer from:

- loss of confidence
- stress
- humiliation
- insomnia
- low morale

- anxiety
- physical sickness
- bad work performance.

You may need time off work and even long-term sickness leave.

And the price to your employer:

- disharmony in the workplace
- unhappy workers
- reduced output
- reduced profits
- high sickness levels.

And if found guilty of race discrimination damages are unlimited.

What the law says

The legal definition:

Race discrimination occurs when a person is treated less favourably on the grounds of race, colour, nationality, ethnic or national origin.

It is unlawful to discriminate against any worker on racial grounds. The Race Relations Act 1976 (RRC76) makes it unlawful to discriminate in:

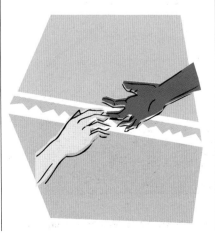

- recruitment
- pay (including bonuses and shift premiums)
- other terms and conditions (e.g. holidays)
- access to opportunities or benefits (e.g. promotion, training, bonuses)
- dismissal
- or by disadvantaging a worker in any other way on racial grounds.

There are three different kinds of discrimination forbidden by law.

1) Direct discrimination occurs when a worker is treated less favourably on the grounds of race, colour, nationality, ethnic or national origin. Direct discrimination is relatively easy to identify but can be more difficult to prove.

2) Indirect discrimination is more complicated and can be difficult to prove in a court or tribunal. Indirect discrimination flows from some condition put on applicants for a job if the condition:

- is likely to lead to preference being given to one or more racial group rather than others;
- it cannot be justified by the requirements of the job.

To explain this further it is best to take an example. If a condition in a job ad was that all applicants must have high standards of spoken English then it would clearly discriminate against non-native English speakers. But if the job was working in a call-centre, good spoken English is needed to do the job properly. This would not therefore be indirect discrimination. But if the ad were for a job on an assembly line, it would be likely to be indirect discrimination because you do not need high standards of spoken English to operate routine machinery.

Many cases are not as clear-cut as this, and you will need expert advice if you think you are suffering from indirect discrimination.

3) Victimisation is straightforward and occurs if you are treated less

favourably because you have taken action under the Race Relations Act.

Instructions to discriminate

Any manager who tells someone to discriminate on racial grounds, or pressurises them in any other way to do so is breaking the law. If you are victimised in some way because you do not follow an instruction to discriminate (as it is known in legal jargon) then you are likely to have a strong case to take to an Employment Tribunal. Take advice.

Who is legally liable?

The discrimination you face at work might flow from the actions of your workmates rather than your boss. But your employer is still legally liable. They are responsible for ensuring that there is no racism in the workplace.

In legal jargon this is known as 'vicarious liability'. The employer can only avoid taking the blame if he or she can show that they have taken reasonable practical steps to prevent discrimination. This should include taking disciplinary action against anyone guilty of racist behaviour.

Your employer has a general duty to provide a safe and healthy workplace. If there is bullying of any kind, or other behaviour which affects your health or ability to do your job, you may be able to use the law to make your employer change their approach.

But individual employees can also be held legally responsible.

An employee who knowingly discriminates against another employee or applicant on the grounds of race, or who aids discriminatory practices, is acting unlawfully. The Commission for Racial Equality's Code of Practice states that employees have a duty to comply with measures introduced by their employer to ensure equality of opportunity and non-discrimination.

What to do if you have suffered discrimination

While this article stresses your legal rights, going to law is not always the best way to resolve problems and you should always take advice at an early stage. Court or tribunal cases can be stressful and while we encourage people to stand up for their rights, you should think through carefully what you want to do. You can win compensation but it will not necessarily be the kind of large figures sometimes reported in newspapers. The average settlement in a race discrimination case at an Employment Tribunal is £5,000.

These are some of the steps you may take:

- Talk to colleagues who might be suffering the same problems. If they are, work out together what you want to do about them. Talk to friends who might have suffered similar problems where they work. It's always helpful to share a problem and trying to cope with pressure on your own can be particularly stressful.
- Keep a diary of events of who said what, when, circumstances and any witnesses. This will give a vital record of the nature of racism.
- Find out whether your employer has specific rules about racism at work or a grievance procedure you can use to raise a problem. Since the summer of 2000 the law has changed to allow you to bring a colleague or trade union officer with you to such hearings. Good employers already do.

- If you are in a union, contact your union rep or shop steward to assist you with talking to management or approaching any harasser.
- If your local union rep is unable to help, then contact your local union officer responsible for equality matters, the equality officer, in the union's head office or a member of the union's race relations committee or group. (Different unions will have different structures.)
- If there is no trade union at your workplace contact the TUC know your rights telephone line on 0870 6004 882 to find the one that is most appropriate.
- The TUC know your rights line can also provide leaflets on other workplace issues such as bullying, and a general leaflet on your job and the law which explains how employment tribunals work.
- The Commission for Racial Equality is a national body that can help victims of race discrimination.
- Your local Citizens' Advice Bureau or Law Centre may be able to help. You can get their details from the phone book or a local library.
- You may want to talk to a private solicitor – although you should be aware that it is very unusual to be awarded costs in an employment tribunal. The Law Society can provide a list of law firms that specialise in discrimination issues.

- The above information is reprinted with kind permission from the Trades Union Congress. Please visit www.tuc.org.uk for more information or see page 41 for details.
© TUC

Discrimination in employment

New figures released show employers continue to discriminate, unabated

New figures released by equality organisation C2e say that up to 1.1 million employers discriminate in the selection and recruitment of candidates. C2e says the Government must get its act together.

Committed 2 Equality (C2e) is a not-for-profit organisation that works with businesses to help develop and implement equality policies.

According to figures released from C2e last week, although many large corporations say that they have sound equality policies in place, in reality few actually do.

Only 23% of large companies in the UK have equality procedures in place and in small companies the situation is even worse – 97.5% have no equality practices in place at all.

C2e maintain that one in ten of the UK population are job seekers – 3.5 million people.

Ethnic minorities are the most discriminated against when it comes to gaining employment, finding it twice as difficult to secure work.

The unemployed amount to 1.4 million but there are a further 2.1 million (150% more) who are not classified as unemployed but who are willing to work.

According to C2e most companies overlook the benefits to their businesses when good equality practices are in place.

CEO of C2e Janet Lakhani told Black Britain:

'If an organisation has equality practices in place the numbers show that they employ more individuals from a disadvantaged background.

'Equally organisations who have little in the way of equality practices employ fewer individuals from disadvantaged backgrounds.'

'Disadvantaged' in this context refers to disadvantaged by race, disability and single-parent status.

These include more customers, more profits, an expanded labour pool and better business performance.

However, the latest estimates suggest that around 1.1 million companies are discriminating in the way that they select and recruit new employees.

Public organisations have a legal obligation to promote equality. However, few are meeting this obligation.

Only 23% of large companies in the UK have equality procedures in place and in small companies the situation is even worse

---

A related survey showed that not one local authority that replied to a questionnaire even bother to ask whether any of their 600,000 suppliers have equality practices in place after contracts are awarded.

Janet Lakhani, the CEO of C2e, said:

'The Government already has the power to tackle this, but it needs to get its act together – many disadvantaged individuals are willing to work – what is needed are businesses willing to employ.'
4 October 2005

■ The above information is reprinted with kind permission from Black Britain , part of the Colourful Network. For more information please visit www.blackbritain.co.uk or to write to them, please see page 41 for their address details.

© *The Colourful Network*

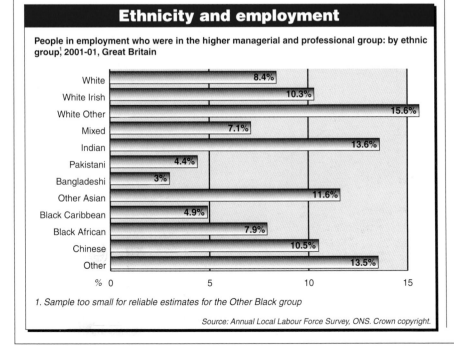

Ethnicity and employment

People in employment who were in the higher managerial and professional group: by ethnic group¹, 2001-01, Great Britain

Ethnic group	%
White	8.4%
White Irish	10.3%
White Other	15.6%
Mixed	7.1%
Indian	13.6%
Pakistani	4.4%
Bangladeshi	3%
Other Asian	11.6%
Black Caribbean	4.9%
Black African	7.9%
Chinese	10.5%
Other	13.5%

1. Sample too small for reliable estimates for the Other Black group

Source: Annual Local Labour Force Survey, ONS. Crown copyright.

Racism in the workplace

Workplace racism denies training to many qualified black workers

Racism in Britain's workplaces is damaging the career prospects of many black workers because at every level of working life they get less training opportunities, despite often being better qualified than their white counterparts.

A new TUC report launched today (Friday 15 April) to coincide with the TUC's annual Black Workers' conference entitled 'Workplace training – a race for opportunity', reveals that even though job-related training is more likely to be offered to qualified workers, qualified black and minority ethnic workers (BME) receive less opportunities.

The report shows that 28 per cent of BMEs are graduates, compared to just 20 per cent of white workers. And while having a degree significantly increases access to job-related training, only 17 per cent of white graduates have never been offered training, compared to 20 per cent of black workers.

But where BME workers are employed in workplaces with trade union recognition, or are in the public sector the openings to training are much improved. The positive actions taken by unions, and imposed by the Race Relations Amendment Act (2000) on employers have limited the effects of workplace racism.

Brendan Barber, TUC General Secretary, said: 'Racism at work is still preventing too many black workers from fulfilling their potential. We need new legislation that will force all employers to give equal access to training for all workers. The TUC is campaigning to extend Britain's race relations law to make all workplaces respond positively to the training needs of black workers.'

Certain ethnic groups, in particular Pakistani and Bangladeshi employees, face real barriers to training opportunities. Nearly two-fifths (39 per cent) of Pakistani

employees and nearly half (47 per cent) of Bangladeshi employees have never been offered training. And in the case of Bangladeshi men, this rises to more than half (51 per cent).

Main findings from 'Workplace training – a race for opportunity'

- Some 31 per cent of BME workers have never been offered training by their current employer. This compares with 29 per cent of white employees not being offered training.
- Public sector employees are much more likely to be offered training by their employer. Only 15 per cent of BME public sector employees say they have never been offered training, compared to 37 per cent working in the private sector. The equivalent figures for white employees are 14 per cent and 35 per cent.

- Those belonging to a trade union have a huge advantage in being offered training. Just 16 per cent of unionised BME employees have never been offered training compared to 36 per cent who are not union members.
- In certain industrial sectors there is a clear divide in equality of access to training. For example, in manufacturing nearly half (48 per cent) of BME employees say that they have never been offered training compared to only 37 per cent of white employees.
- The 'qualification divide' has a huge impact on who is offered job-related training by their employer. For the workforce at large, there is a clear 'training hierarchy' with only 17 per cent of employees with a degree saying that they have never been offered such training compared to 55 per cent of those employees without any qualifications.

11 April 2005

- The above information is reprinted with kind permission from the Trades Union Congress. Please visit www.tuc.org.uk for more information or see page 41 for details.

© TUC

Black History Month

Frequently asked questions

Why was Black History Month established and what is the aim?

Best encapsulated in these memorable words from Ken Livingstone at the Royal Albert Hall,

'In order to further enrich the cultural diversity of the Greater London area, it is imperative that Londoners know more about African influences on medieval and renaissance European music and more about the roots of Greek music so that accepted ideas about European music are changed. Despite the significant role that Africa and its Diaspora has played in the world civilisation since the beginning of time, Africa's contribution has been omitted or distorted in most history books.'

The halls of the GLC were opened to the community, and to internationally renowned musicians such as Max Roach, Hugh Masekela, Burning Spear, Courtney Pine, Abdullah Ibrahim, Tania Maria, and artistes from the USA, Caribbean, Africa, Ireland and India.

There were many people involved during this period of expansion in our community who all helped to establish the programme. Hopefully, we recognise these people's collective contribution, not listed in any particular order: Ansel Wong, Paul Boateng, Ken Livingstone, Pat Gordon, Bernie Grant, Lord Gifford, Anne Mathews, Vitus Evans, Margaret Hodge, Ken Martindale, Shirley Andrews, Linda Bellos, Narenda Makenji, Chris Boothman, Pat Lamour and Edward Oteng.

Activities of children filling the Royal Albert Hall for a week led to the thinking 'if it has been initiated, why not institutionalise it?', so the idea of Black History Month was born.

What form do events take and where are they held?

Events take place the length and breadth of the country 17 years on, with circa 3,000 events this year. It must be noted that some of these events have catalysed the way that the cultural services are disseminated throughout the year.

Voluntary organisations, local authorities, museums, libraries and archives have started to take the lead in art planning as soon as one year is over and one could argue that it would seem that they are able, through excellent and skilled professionals, experts and resources, to marshal and lever support from large funders. Not forgetting the smaller groups, who do excellent work e.g. running supplementary schools, which incorporate history. Wales for example launched their programme last week.

There is a richness and diversity of programmers who plan imaginative and thought-provoking events, storytelling, walks, theatrical productions, comedy and the first Black History Month Ball, all having history as an integral part of the productions. This year (2004) some of the more grassroots organisers, rightly so, are recognising the importance of the Pan Caribbean hurricane disaster and are incorporating fundraising activities.

Local authorities, where they can earmark specific budgets, encourage groups to apply at the beginning of each financial year. There are small amounts, with some councils picking up and absorbing publicity and venue hire in some cases.

There is also growth in large museums working alongside and sharing marketing and promotions

Why do black people need a history month?

In an ideal world, we wouldn't need the month, as education establishments will fully recognise and appreciate our contribution to history. It is important as well to have the political will in the first place which was around during its inception.

We need a history month, as our opportunity to share with the world at large our incredible contribution to this planet. We need a history month so that we all can be proud of our creativity, respect our intellectual prowess and celebrate our culture whether it be in the way we walk, shoulders back, head up high, or whether we are purchasing books, pamphlets and magazines from our community.

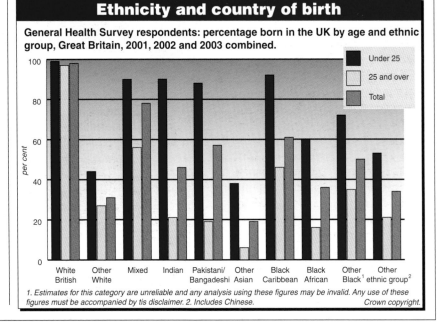

Ethnicity and country of birth

General Health Survey respondents: percentage born in the UK by age and ethnic group, Great Britain, 2001, 2002 and 2003 combined.

1. Estimates for this category are unreliable and any analysis using these figures may be invalid. Any use of these figures must be accompanied by tis disclaimer. 2. Includes Chinese. Crown copyright.

cost. E.g. the South Kensington group consisting of V&A, Natural History Museum, Royal Geographical Society and the Science Museum.

What date does it start and when does it end? And why October?

1st-31st October.

We are seeing a growth in events starting now from mid-September till mid-November.

The concern in the UK about the children, our future generation, was crucial to our decision-making. October is also very significant within the African cultural calendar – the period of the Autumn equinox in Africa is consecrated as the harvest period, the period of plenty, the period of the Yam festivals.

Apart from that, October is a period of tolerance and recon-

'Despite the significant role that Africa has played in world civilization, its contribution has been omitted or distorted in most history books'

ciliation in African; it is a period of the coming together of the various bodies that entailed the African societies, the Kingdoms. Black History is therefore a reconnection with our source, hence the chosen symbol of Sankofa – learning from the past, with the benefit of hindsight.

October is more or less the beginning of the school year, young people have had a long summer break, their minds are refreshed, and

they are not saddled so much with homework or examinations. That was why October was chosen.

Who celebrates it? Can anyone participate, or is just for Black people?

Black History month is open to participation by everyone and is ideally developed, delivered and managed as an educational and historical awareness experience by Black people – the African Heritage experience should be shared by everyone as world history.

Sourced with permission from New African October Magazine - Akyaaba Addai Sebo, former worker at the GLC.

■ Reprinted with permission from Mia Morris Well Placed Consultancy. Visit www.black-history-month.co.uk or see page 41.

© *Black History Month*

Black history and education

Baroness says black history should be integrated into Britain's education and not confined to one month

As Black History Month knocks on our doors once again this year, Baroness Amos tells Black Britain that the positive contribution of black people shouldn't be confined to just one month but should be integrated into British education and culture.

As Britain's communities prepare to attend the hundreds of different events to celebrate this year's Black History Month, many are questioning whether the positive contribution made by the country's black communities should solely be pegged to the month of October instead of being ingested by the British society as a whole.

Many educationalists have gestured that integrating positive black history into the national school curriculum is a way of educating and waking up the consciousness of today's youth to the positive contribution black people

have made to British and world history.

With the Prime Minster calling for education to be put at the heart of the country's agenda at last week's Brighton conference, the Leader of the House of Lords, Baroness Valerie Amos, spoke to Black Britain about the significance of celebrating black achievement in order to progress as a community.

Agreeing that more positive episodes of black history should be acknowledged in schools rather than the black contribution to British history being limited to slavery, she told Black Britain at the conference:

'I think it's really important that we celebrate our achievement so that we celebrate our important role models . . . I think that as a community we need to be much more confident and positive about that.'

She added, 'There are a lot of people within our communities who are constantly looking back to colonial history [and] to slavery; I think we have to recognise the reality of our history and what it did in terms of our communities, but I think we also have to look forward and celebrate our achievement.'

As one of the very few black faces present in parliament, the Baroness, who was appointed as leader of the House of Lords in 2003, said that events such as Black History Month do bear importance as it raises awareness of 'our history' and also 'what that history has done in terms of the contribution that we all now make'.

Nonetheless, she added: 'I would be very sad indeed if I thought that the only way these issues could get raised and aired was through one month in a year.'

She explained that through the government's wider citizenship agenda, these issues should be discussed in our schools through sections of the curriculum which relate to citizenship and history as well as through our communities.

The teaching of black history in schools is left to the discretion of the teachers.

With the emphasis of Britain's diverse society being a focus for Tony Blair's government, Jacquie Smith, the Minister for Schools, told Black Britain that when reviewing the education system in 1999, it was noticed that there were more opportunities to 'use' positive role models to positively reinforce the contribution of the black community through the education system.

There are still no plans for the government to cement black history in the current curriculum but Ms Smith added that 'there's a limited amount that you do through the curriculum' and that it is up to the individual teacher to incorporate more positive histories into the curriculum for their pupils to benefit.

'We don't have the kind of national curriculum that lays down precisely what you teach and at what point you teach that.'

She said the government had laid down some 'important principles' in relation to citizenship to give schools the 'important opportunity to address issues particularly around discrimination [and] the diversity of the society we live in'.

Ms Smith also said the government had also supported and encouraged teachers to take up elements of this month's celebration as a chance to teach pupils about black history in the classroom.

'I know that Black History Month is well taken up by schools as a way of getting positive messages about the contribution of black communities around the UK and positive histories into schools.'

Knowing black history would help pupils to understand the richness of Britain's multi-cultural society, Baroness Amos said. Although the roots of black children under-achieving is 'complex', teaching all pupils about black history could help

Knowing black history would help pupils to understand the richness of Britain's multi-cultural society

them understand Britain's diverse society. However, leaving education on the positive role of black people's past and present contribution to the British history books up to teachers leads some to question whether this is the most constructive way of ensuring that black history is acknowledged and understood by pupils.

With an education system which has been seen as failing many black pupils, there is some cynicism as to whether leaving it up to the teacher's discretion to follow through with teaching positive black history instead of making it a permanent feature of the curriculum will work.

Although Baroness Amos acknowledged that the reason for some black pupils not achieving has 'its roots in many factors', she said the purpose of teaching black history isn't just about benefiting black and ethnic minority children, but she said, 'It is about us having an understanding as a multi-heritage society.'

She said Britain's social make-up is what gives the country its complexity and 'some of the challenges and tensions that we have to face precisely around that diversity agenda'.

Baroness Amos said, 'Our young people are experiencing it on a day-to-day basis in terms of how they live their lives, how they build relationships with others, how they interact with each other.'

She added, 'I think all of our children need to have a better understanding of that history, that diversity, that richness [and] that context which make up who we are in Britain today.'

Scharene Pryce, 3 October 2005

■ Printed with permission of Black Britain (www.blackbritain.co.uk), part of the Colourful Network. For more information see page 41.

© *The Colourful Network*

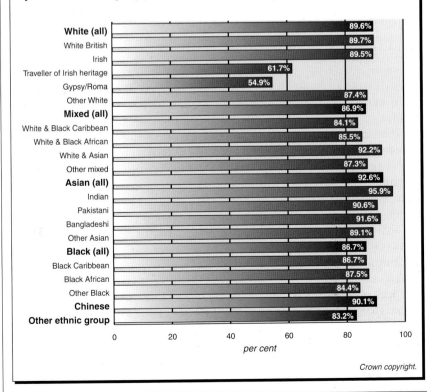

GCSE achievement by ethnicity

Achievements at GCSE and equivalent in 2004 by ethnicity: percentage fifteen-year-olds achieving any passes

Ethnicity	per cent
White (all)	89.6%
White British	89.7%
Irish	89.5%
Traveller of Irish heritage	61.7%
Gypsy/Roma	54.9%
Other White	87.4%
Mixed (all)	86.9%
White & Black Caribbean	84.1%
White & Black African	85.5%
White & Asian	92.2%
Other mixed	87.3%
Asian (all)	92.6%
Indian	95.9%
Pakistani	90.6%
Bangladeshi	91.6%
Other Asian	89.1%
Black (all)	86.7%
Black Caribbean	86.7%
Black African	87.5%
Other Black	84.4%
Chinese	90.1%
Other ethnic group	83.2%

Crown copyright.

Ethnicity and education

The evidence on minority ethnic pupils – key findings

- In 2004, 17 per cent of the maintained school population in England was classified as belonging to a minority ethnic group.
- The minority ethnic school population (maintained schools) has grown by an estimated fifth to a third in number since 1997; in comparison, there has been a much smaller increase of 2.3 per cent in the total number of pupils in maintained schools during the same period.
- Indian, Chinese , White/Asian and Irish pupils are more likely to gain five or more A*-C GCSEs compared to other ethnic groups. Gypsy/Roma pupils, Travellers of Irish Heritage, Black Caribbean and White/Black Caribbean pupils are amongst the lower achieving pupils at Key Stage 4.
- Although numbers recorded in these ethnic categories are small, it is clear that Gypsy/Roma pupils and Travellers of Irish Heritage have very low attainment throughout Key Stage assessments and also have much higher identification of special educational needs.
- A large proportion of Gypsy/ Roma pupils and Travellers of Irish Heritage appear to drop out of secondary school. Only a third of the number of pupils are registered on the Annual School Census as Gypsy/Roma at Key Stage 4 compared to Key Stage 1; and less than a half of pupils are registered as Travellers of Irish Heritage at Key Stage 4 compared to Key Stage 1.
- Travellers of Irish Heritage are the lowest achieving group at Key Stages 1 and 2. Of those Gypsy/ Roma pupils attending secondary schools, they are the lowest achieving group at Key Stages 3 and 4. Only 23 per cent of Gypsy/ Roma pupils achieved 5+ A*-C GCSEs in 2003 (compared to the 51 per cent national average).
- Attainment data on Mixed Heritage pupils shows that White/Asian pupils are amongst the highest achieving ethnic groups (with 65 per cent attaining 5+ A*-C GCSEs compared to the 51 per cent national figure) and that White/Black Caribbean pupils have lower achievement than the average (40 per cent attaining 5+ A*-C GCSEs).
- Black Caribbean and Black Other boys are twice as likely to have been categorised as having behavioural, emotional or social difficulty as White British boys (identified as a special educational need type of School Action Plus or statement).
- Pakistani pupils are two to five times more likely than White British pupils to have an identified visual impairment or hearing impairment (identified as a special educational need of School Action Plus or statement).
- Pupils with English as an additional language are slightly less likely to be identified with a special educational need (7.2 per cent compared to 8.3 per cent of pupils with English as a first language) and are less likely to be classified as having a specific learning difficulty, behaviour, emotional and social difficulties or an autistic spectrum disorder. However, they are more likely to have an identified speech, language or communication need.
- Permanent exclusion rates are higher than average for Travellers of Irish Heritage, Gypsy/Roma, Black Caribbean, Black Other and White/Black Caribbean pupils.
- Within the Excellence in Cities initiative, Black Caribbean and Black African pupils were more likely than other groups to have reported seeing a Learning Mentor. Minority ethnic pupils were less likely than White pupils to be identified for the Gifted and Talented strand of the programme.
- In Excellence in Cities areas, Black Other pupils have higher rates of unauthorised absence than other pupils. White pupils have higher rates of authorised absence than Black Caribbean, Indian, Bangladeshi, Black African or Chinese pupils.

- Just over half (53 per cent) of parents/carers of minority ethnic children reported feeling very involved with their child's education, a much greater proportion than the 38 per cent of a representative sample of all parents who reported this.
- Nine per cent of teachers teaching in England are from a minority ethnic group. In London, this figure rises to 31 per cent.

- Information from key findings of *Ethnicity and Education: The Evidence on Minority Ethnic Pupils*, from the Department for Education and Skills. Visit www.dfes.gov.uk for more information or to view the full report.
  © Crown copyright

Why black kids fail at school

Information from Black Information Link

A hardhitting new education report has lifted the lid on a culture of racism in schools which holds black pupils back.

Research by the Joseph Rowntree Foundation showed that Britain's education system continues to suppress black achievement by having low expectations of black pupils.

Thousands of African-Caribbean children excluded from school are forced to rely on help from poorly-funded community groups to continue their education.

According to the study, excluded youngsters turned to voluntary organisations, family and friends to help them turn their lives around.

Limbo

Racism played a part in exclusions, with black pupils believing they were punished more severely than their white peers for the same behaviour problems.

One Nottingham pupil, Richard, 18, told researchers: 'If I was white I might have got away with it.'

Seventeen-year-old Lucinda from London said: 'I think it's because I'm black, especially how the other

By Shirin Aguiar-Holloway

[white] girl was allowed back to school the next day.'

Earl, 18, from Nottingham, said: 'They play the white kids against the black ones, being a white child or something, the black child gets in trouble for it and the white child gets away with it, you see them do it and the black child gets in trouble for it.'

Trapped

The new research, entitled *School Exclusion and Transition into Adulthood in African-Caribbean Communities*, added: 'The young people in this study felt trapped by the white teachers' and white pupils' low expectations and understanding of black culture.

'They stereotyped black students as aggressive, athletic and oversized.'

Exclusions figures show that on average black pupils are four times more likely to be excluded than their white counterparts.

The study found that only 15 per cent of permanently-excluded youngsters are reintegrated into mainstream school.

The rest were left in 'educational limbo' without any immediate alternative to school. The report will merely confirm what has been known for a long time in the black community.

Gloria Hyatt, Liverpool-based education consultant, said the issues raised were 'old, long and established problems that are yet to be adequately accepted or addressed by statutory providers'.

Foretaste

Harsher punishments at school 'made them conscious of the fact that race would affect the way they were seen by others and that the significance of their racial identity in their experience of exclusion was very likely a foretaste of experiences they would have in wider society'.

Against all the odds, however, most of the excluded pupils interviewed for the research had overcome their exclusion and were studying or working, having used their experience to reassess themselves.

Report co-author Cecile Wright from Nottingham Trent University said that while being excluded had been traumatic for youngsters, leading to a loss of dignity and self-respect, for most it didn't stop there.

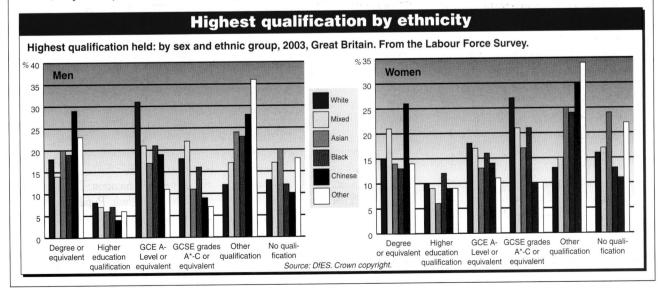

Highest qualification by ethnicity

Highest qualification held: by sex and ethnic group, 2003, Great Britain. From the Labour Force Survey.

Source: DfES. Crown copyright.

'In most cases it was followed by the development of a resilient sense of self and a positive black identity that motivated young people to disprove low official expectations and prove their worth.

Averting

'But it was families and dedicated workers in community-based groups, usually depending on short-term funding, who had helped young people to make that critical change in their lives.'

Key recommendations are for the government to provide guidance and training in averting school exclusions and to fund training of all those involved in the exclusion process.

The study, launched at the House of Commons, was based on in-depth interviews with 33 African-Caribbean youngsters aged from 14 to 19 in London and Nottingham who had been excluded from school.

Hyatt blasted local education authorities (LEAs) and the Government for failing black pupils, adding: 'Whilst I think it is good that the LEA want to retain excluded pupils within mainstream provision, they are failing these pupils by the level of unacceptable provision that is currently available.

'There is little encouragement for schools to retain these pupils and more rationale and pressure to exclude, leaving the majority isolated and with little hope of ever returning.'

A Department for Education and Skills spokesman said: 'We fully back heads that take tough action to tackle misbehaviour and disruption in the classroom, permanently excluding pupils where their behaviour warrants it.'
14 September 2005

■ Information from Black Information Link. For more information, visit www.blink.org.uk
© Black Information Link

Boosting Black achievement

Innovative scheme to boost achievement for Black pupils goes national

An innovative scheme to boost achievement amongst Black pupils will be rolled out nationally to 84 schools in 20 Local Authorities from this year, Schools Minister Andrew Adonis announced today (7 October 2005).

The Black Pupils' Achievement Programme aims to increase success among Black pupils through a tailored leadership and management strategy that aims to boost effective teaching and learning, tackle poor behaviour and bullying, introduce mentoring and increase the involvement of parents. Each school appoints a member of the senior leadership team to draw up an action plan to drive forward these changes. The programme follows the success of the African-Caribbean Achievement Project piloted in 30 schools across England from November 2003.

Welcoming the national roll-out, Schools Minister Andrew Adonis said:

'The underachievement of Black pupils, and boys in particular, is a serious issue'

'The underachievement of Black pupils, and boys in particular, is a serious issue for this Government and one on which we are focusing our attention and resources.

'As a result we are already seeing some improvements. Last year Black pupils achieved the greatest rate of improvement in GCSEs. Black Caribbean pupils' 5 A*-C pass rate went up by 2.8 percentage points to 35.7 per cent, and Black African pupils rose by 2.6 percentage points to 43.3 per cent against a national average increase of 1.2 percentage points to 51.9 per cent for all pupils.

'These results show that Black pupils are now closing the attainment gap and our strategies are delivering year-on-year improvements. But the gap is still far too wide – this programme is just one part of the Government's commitment to improving attainment to make sure that all pupils reach their full potential.

'The experience of these pilots has shown that the project has been highly effective in providing examples of good practice which can be used in other schools. I'm pleased that across the 30 pilot schools, a host of ideas to get parents and the local community involved have been developed.'

Notes

This press notice relates to 'England'

1. The African Caribbean Achievement Project's final evaluation report is not due until early 2006, but it is clear from the emerging findings that the project has been highly effective in providing examples of good practice.

2. Cost of pilot projects was £1.7m over two years and roll-out is approximately £1.3m a year.

3. The Statistical First Release 'National Curriculum Assessment, GCSE and equivalent attainment and Post-16 attainment by pupil characteristics, in England, 2004' is available at: http://www.dfes.gov.uk/rsgateway/DB/SFR/s000564/index.shtml
7 October 2005

■ The above information is reprinted with kind permission from the Department for Education and Skills. For more information please visit the DfES website at www.dfes.gov.uk
© Crown copyright

Black boys 'do better in a class of their own'

Teaching black boys separately could help them learn more quickly, according to a leading black American academic.

Dr Stan Mims told a conference in London staged by Trevor Phillips, chairman of the Commission for Racial Equality, about the success of the idea in the US.

Only 31.9 per cent of black boys managed five A to C passes last year against a national average of 51.9 per cent

Mr Phillips has been accused of promoting 'educational apartheid' for supporting the use of the measure in Britain.

But he says it could address under-achievement in GCSEs by black boys, only 31.9 per cent of whom managed five A to C passes last year against a national average of 51.9 per cent. Dr Mims introduced the policy of separating black boys from other pupils for English, maths and

By Laura Clark, Education Reporter

science when he took control of the education department of East St Louis, Illinois, last year.

Boys were pulled out of lessons if they were identified as struggling in one or more of the disciplines.

Dr Mims said that, as a result, the pupils had begun to make considerable improvements.

'We pull black boys out based on their ability to master certain skills,' he said.

'They are not separated in terms of the entire school. They are only pulled out in their school based on certain mastery of literacy or numeracy or science.

'By doing that we are able to support them with the skills they need to pass high-stakes exams.'

He said there had been 'large gains' in local examinations this year, but stressed that success depended on parental support.

'We have to educate our parents about the rationale for doing such a

programme, then we are able to get the students to opt in,' he said.

The measure was allied with recruitment campaigns to attract high-calibre black teachers.

Mr Phillips has been accused of promoting 'educational apartheid'

Dr Mims insisted the students involved said they did not feel stigmatised or that they were being treated differently because of their race. He said his department faced penalties under US law if they failed to educate the children.

But Mr Phillips's suggestion that the idea be tried in Britain brought an angry reaction from teachers, parents and education experts, who said it raised the spectre of segregation.

Black academic Dr Tony Sewell, also present at yesterday's seminar, said the policy could cause 'resentment and division in schools'.

Mr Phillips warned that poor exam results among black boys risked turning them into a 'permanent underclass'.

He added that their educational failure could not simply be blamed on racism among teachers.

■ This article first appeared in the *Daily Mail*, 2 June 2005.

© 2005 Associated Newspapers Ltd

Breaking stereotypes

'Reality TV' catalyst for integration and breaking ethnic minority stereotypes, says CRE chair Trevor Phillips – information reprinted with permission from the Commission for Racial Equality

'Reality TV' is the media phenomenon which has done more for racial and ethnic understanding than any other media creation in recent years, Trevor Phillips, CRE Chair, will say this evening at the Commission for Racial Equality's (CRE) Race in the Media Awards (RIMA).

Speaking from the Curzon Cinema, Mayfair, Trevor Phillips, CRE Chair, will say:

'Until very recently most people's idea of what a black or Asian or Chinese or Gypsy person is really like is almost entirely based on what they read, hear and see in the media and has been very stereotyped. But so called "reality TV" has given many British people a chance to encounter people from other ethnic groups they would never meet in their own everyday lives.

'And I don't suppose that the Big Brother house is most people's idea of any kind of reality. But in Kamal the bisexual Muslim; Derek, the world's poshest black man and Makosi the feminist Zimbabwean nurse, we have three people who would confound any possible stereo-typing.

'Most encouragingly, according to the man behind Big Brother, Peter Bazalgette, the evidence is that the voters do not line up in any way – that is to say they seem completely uninfluenced by issues of race and ethnicity in deciding who they want to chuck out or keep in.

'Take The Apprentice where the final four contestants all came from immigrant backgrounds. The winner, Tim Campbell, in spite of being a black man, who grew up with a single parent, turned up to work on time and was at last someone who wasn't a one dimensional 'bad ways' black man.

'"Reality TV" has also shown that non-white folks can be just as individualistic as anyone else. We can defy our own historical stereotypes. Young British people are increasingly demonstrating that they can respect the culture of their parents without having to adopt it wholesale. For example who could ever dare to ask British Asian women to be sweet, submissive and silent, after watching The Apprentice's Saira Khan in action?'

The 2005 RIMA ceremony includes 16 categories, covering television, radio, print, film and new media. Winners will be those who, in the opinion of the independent judges, have made a significant contribution to public appreciation and understanding of multiculturalism, diversity or race relations.
28 June 2005

■ The above information is reprinted with kind permission from the Commission for Racial Equality. Visit www.cre.gov.uk for more or see page 41 for address details.
© Commission for Racial Equality

Mixed blessings

You are more likely in Britain to fall in love with someone of another race than anywhere else in the world. And yet last week a black teenager, out with his white girlfriend, was murdered. Katharina Lobeck, whose partner is Senegalese, says mixed-race couples never escape being judged.

It's hard to imagine a more horrific murder than that of Anthony Walker. Bludgeoned to death with an axe for having committed no crime other than that of sitting on a bench with his white girlfriend. This isn't supposed to happen in modern Britain, a country that prides itself in being one of the most diverse nations of the world. It shouldn't happen six years after the Stephen Lawrence inquiry forced British society to tackle the racism that had shown itself to be endemic in many of its institutions and community groups. But it did happen, and will have this country look at itself once more.

I am a German woman, a Londoner by choice like so many people in this city. I am engaged to be married to a Senegalese man, and the mother of his child. For me, news of Friday's race attack felt like another brutal sign telling me to try my luck elsewhere, another menac-ing message from (and to) multi-cultural Britain. Not only because an axe-swinging psychopath com-mitted a race crime, but also because, once again, multiculturalism and mixed-race relationships find them-selves under investigation as a result.

My partner and I have now spent two years trying to find a way for him to move to London permanently. He still hasn't been able to obtain a long-term visa; the chances are that we might have had a much easier ride in Germany. And yet, I didn't manage to tear myself away from London. (Having spent some time in Bristol and in other communities in the UK, I do believe that the capital's multicultural spirit is unique among British cities.) Despite its dismal living conditions, its extortionate rents, despite its general aggressiveness and its never-fulfilling promise of success, London seemed to be the only place I could imagine living in. The only place where I felt my (at the time single) motherhood to a mixed-race child and my relationship with an African man could pass, not unnoticed, but without being permanently commented upon. It seemed to be the only place where we would not be reduced to being a hideous cliché and, above all, where we would run a relatively low risk of being harassed. I believe that's still the case, even though Saturday's race attack in Liverpool forces Britain to ask itself some questions.

When I considered leaving London with my child, my home nation Germany was an obvious option to consider. Except that it wasn't. In Germany, even a third

generation of immigrants is not seen, and often does not see itself, as being German, and the idea of a non-white German is still a completely alien one to large parts of the population. There, comments about our 'chocolate baby' or 'negro doll' have accompanied me and my partner ever since my daughter was born. Neighbours visiting my parents to congratulate them on their first grandchild also warned them of the perils of accepting an African son-in-law into the family fold.

Then there was Paris, the place of choice for many Senegalese expatriates. Stories from friends about race-motivated evictions and the reported impossibilities of finding flats for mixed-race couples discouraged us. In Dakar, I hadn't been able to find work. London, with its promise of cultural diversity, seemed the only place where we'd be able to blend in. Praising London as one of the great multicultural capitals of the world may sound like verbal floss taken from the mayor's campaign book, but it is London reality, even though there remain many contradictions and confrontations involved in having a multitude of ethnic, faith and cultural groups sitting side by side in one sprawling conurbation.

It's when I walk with my daughter through Brixton market that I get the most questioning, and occasionally menacing, stares, mainly from black women. If I'm with my partner, he gets them, from his male peers. On my own, I look like the archetype of the greedy white woman; the one who got off with a black man, ended up with a child – and now look what you got for it. If we're together, he looks like a traitor to the black community, someone likely to have got involved with a white girl to 'have it easy'. This somewhat understandable wariness on behalf of parts of the black community can be even greater when it comes to couples of black women and white men, still the less public face of mixed-race Britain. An east African friend of mine calls it the 'protective spirit of the minority', born from defiance and dignity.

Ronnie McGrath, a black British writer, has also experienced animos-

ity from both sides. Fifteen to 20 years ago, he tells me, he was still being chased regularly by white youngsters for holding a white woman's hand. This kind of wide-scale, open violence has decreased, and many of the mixed-race couples I know say that they can't think of any public display of animosity, let alone violence, towards them. 'I don't notice it', says Sarah Gumbo, a white Zimbabwean living in London. 'There are conflicts within the family, but I don't feel judged in public.' And yet the judgement is there. It is just that nowadays, it rarely comes in the form of a violent blow over the head.

Enter a mixed-race relationship, and you may find yourself suddenly confronted with previously unknown prejudice prevailing among close friends and family

---

These days, racist judgement comes in carefully crafted news features, in conversations conducted smilingly. It comes in questions about my partner's virility, about the likelihood of his faithfulness and his assumed musical talent, asked after a few too many glasses of wine. Racial bias exists in this society, and it's something that mixed-race couples have to deal with. Enter a mixed-race relationship, and you may find yourself suddenly confronted with previously unknown prejudice prevailing among close friends and family. You may find that the news will never quite sound the same again – suddenly you catch sight of society's hidden, ugly face. Relationships are hard work. Mixed-race relationships perhaps slightly more so, as outside pressures, different cultural expectations, and family discord can all increase the burden couples have to bear. But they are also just relationships, and, in London at least, they are part of ordinary city life.
■ Some names have been changed.
2 August 2005
© *Guardian Newspapers Ltd 2005*

In the mix

Why Britain is becoming less black and white: Stuart Jeffries examines the changing complexion of Britain

Britain has the highest level of mixed-race relationships in the developed world. According to the 2001 Census of England and Wales, there were 219,000 marriages between people from different ethnic backgrounds – a figure that obviously massively understates the extent of romantic and sexual relationships between people of different races. A study by the Policy Studies Institute estimated that in 1997 half of black men and one-third of black women in relationships had a white partner, and that those proportions may well have increased since. For a country that flatters itself on its tolerance and its ability to adapt itself to a changing ethnic minority makeup, these are heartening figures.

And the products of all these multi-coloured relationships are changing the complexion of modern Britain. The number of mixed-race people grew by more than 75% during the 1990s to around 415,000, 10% of the total ethnic minority population. (Incidentally, it was in the 2001 Census that the mixed-race category was created, partly in response to a long campaign by those opposed to having to tick the box marked 'other'.)

'In Britain a great deal of mixed-race relationships are between working-class people,' says sociologist Professor Richard Berthoud of the Institute of Social and Economic Research at Essex University. 'It's very different in America, where prosperous black men might have white wives, but such relationships are rare.'

Very different indeed. Britain is not the United States, where the last anti-miscegenation law was ruled unconstitutional by the Supreme Court only in 1967, and where continuing social discomfort over mixed-race relationships has been expressed in films such as Spike Lee's *Jungle Fever* (about the difficulties an African-American man and an Italian-American woman face when they start a relationship) and *Guess Who?*, a ghastly 2005 remake of the 1967 film *Guess Who's Coming to Dinner?*, this time featuring a white boy (Ashton Kutcher) meeting his black girlfriend's family. We like to tell ourselves that Britain isn't like that. 'In America, it is possible to assume that unmarried men and women would have chosen someone from the same ethnic group if they had decided to marry,' writes Professor Berthoud in a new paper.

'That assumption is not nearly so credible in Britain.'

Berthoud tells the story of a British couple, a black woman and a white man, checking into an American hotel. 'They were given separate rooms because the woman was assumed to be a singer and the man her manager. There was no other explanation why they would be together,' he says.

It is hard to imagine something like that happening here, certainly not in Britain's great cities. True, the notion of a respectable concept of 'race' is a hot topic, particularly among sociologists, but that should not spoil the happy image of Britain as a country more than unusually comfortable with relationships between people of different colours.

> *While some may see a black boy in public with a white girl as a sign of hope, for others it is a threat to a racially pure society*

Yasmin Alibhai-Brown, author of *Mixed Feelings: The Complex Lives of Mixed-Race Britons*, and herself a woman of Asian origin married to a white man, has said that this trend towards mixed races in Britain seems to her to be unstoppable. 'I hope it makes this country become more comfortable with its hybridity as a national characteristic.'

It is a big hope. While some may see a black boy in public with a white girl as a sign of hope, for others it is a threat to a racially pure society. The point is, though, that in modern Britain, those who seem threatened by such couples would appear to be a dying breed.

Some hope to explain Anthony Walker's murder in part by blaming it on Liverpool, a city that has a

singular and troubled history of race relations, from its historic role in the slave trade to today, where most black Liverpudlians live in Toxteth, a district described by some as a ghetto. 'In Liverpool, I don't think racism has changed one iota,' says Ken Richards, 60, of the Liverpool 8 Law Centre, an advice centre for the Toxteth area. 'When I was a youth I remember that if you wanted to travel outside Liverpool 8, you would need 20 to 30 mates or you would be in for a kicking.'

> ### *It would be folly to overstate Britain's happy hybridity. Inter-ethnic marriages account for only 2% of all marriages in England and Wales*

But maybe what happened in Liverpool on Friday (29 July 2005) could have happened anywhere. Anthony Clarke, the law centre's coordinator, says: 'Liverpool is no different from any British city where there is a large black community. The thing is that racism is fairly constant. I don't think it's disappeared. But what happened on Friday has shocked us all. It's difficult to get your head round it.'

And it would be folly to overstate Britain's happy hybridity. Interethnic marriages account for only 2% of all marriages in England and Wales. Of these, most (198,000) included a white person. In the remaining 21,000 inter-ethnic marriages, both partners were from different minority ethnic backgrounds. And when you analyse those figures, some very important differences between ethnic groups emerge. Berthoud points out that 50% of British born males of Caribbean origin live with white women partners (a figure that includes married couples), compared with 33% of women. The respective figures for Indian men and women are 20% and 10%, while figures for Pakistani or Bangladeshi are, he says, negligible.

'But you need to realise that Caribbeans have very low partner rates by comparison with other ethnic groups. For example, marriage is seen as an essential part of Muslim identity; it's not quite so for Caribbeans. Also, mixed partnerships are acceptable to most Caribbeans. Among Caribbeans who have come here and been here a long time, there's a keenness to be very much part of British society, but among some black youth – who are not dissimilar in this respect to Muslim youth – there's a different tendency, to be proud of their heritage. In that

respect, to marry into a white family is to be disloyal or opportunistic. But it remains true that the number of black British babies who look out of their cot and see two black parents is very small.'

Professor Berthoud says miscegenation has always been a central issue for white racists, while many liberal commentators see cross-cultural relationships as a welcome sign of increasing mutual acceptance between white and black communities. Clearly that increasing mutual acceptance – if there is such a thing – was found wanting in Liverpool on Friday night.

2 August 2005

© *Guardian Newspapers Limited 2005*

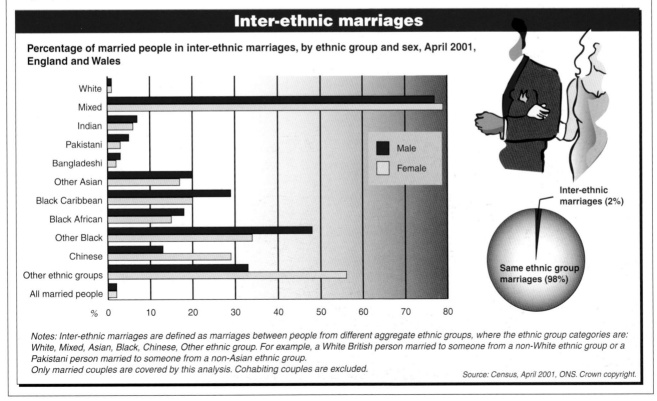

Inter-ethnic marriages

Percentage of married people in inter-ethnic marriages, by ethnic group and sex, April 2001, England and Wales

- Male
- Female

White, Mixed, Indian, Pakistani, Bangladeshi, Other Asian, Black Caribbean, Black African, Other Black, Chinese, Other ethnic groups, All married people

% 0 10 20 30 40 50 60 70 80

Inter-ethnic marriages (2%)

Same ethnic group marriages (98%)

Notes: Inter-ethnic marriages are defined as marriages between people from different aggregate ethnic groups, where the ethnic group categories are: White, Mixed, Asian, Black, Chinese, Other ethnic group. For example, a White British person married to someone from a non-White ethnic group or a Pakistani person married to someone from a non-Asian ethnic group.
Only married couples are covered by this analysis. Cohabiting couples are excluded.

Source: Census, April 2001, ONS. Crown copyright.

Face to faith

The distinction between race and religion is not as clear-cut as our laws on discrimination assume, writes Simon Rocker

Even before July 7, the government had been pressing ahead with its controversial proposal to outlaw incitement to religious hatred. But it would have found further justification in the surge in reported hate crimes, mainly against Muslims, which followed the London bombings.

Supporters of the measure say it is necessary to close a loophole whereby Jews and Sikhs are covered by existing race relations legislation, but Muslims and Buddhists, for example, are not. Someone who whips up animosity against people wearing beards and black hats could face prosecution, but remain immune from it if their target were people wearing hijabs.

Some may feel their religious identity to be more a matter of family ties than theological conviction

According to the government, the intention is to protect members of a religious group from harassment and abuse, not the faith itself from ideological attack. But the bill's numerous adversaries – writers and comedians, as well as politicians – fear it will become a kind of backdoor blasphemy law which will stifle legitimate criticism of religion. And the summer's events seemed to have done little to melt the opposition: several Christian churches are lobbying parliament against the bill on Tuesday.

One of the arguments is that there is a significant difference between legislating on race and on religion. Race, it is said, is an innate characteristic, over which an individual has no choice. Religion, on the other hand, is about ideas and beliefs that are acquired.

In practice, however, this distinction is not quite so clear-cut. The anti-racism laws go beyond biology: as well as colour, they also specify nationality and ethnic origin. It is true that a person has no choice over where they are born, but nationality is partly a cultural and historical construct. Nationality, too, can be exchanged – as, for example, with the sportsmen who are born in one country but play for another.

That Jews are included in the existing provisions also shows some built-in flexibility within the law. Whereas genetic research can now, rather intriguingly, detect markers which bear out the Middle Eastern descent of many of the world's Jews, the research is irrelevant to the law. Jews do not constitute a single racial group. But the law applies equally to a convert to Judaism as to a born Jew, to a Jew originally from Yemen as to a Jew from Lithuania. Their legal protection is surely more to do with history – the knowledge of their persecution in Europe, where anti-Semitism mutated from a religious into a racial form.

When it comes to religious affiliation, it is too abstract to think of this simply in terms of a package of beliefs which can be adopted or discarded at will. Members of a faith group are born into a community, rather than a set of doctrines. Some may feel their religious identity to be more a matter of family ties than theological conviction. A person may feel affinity with a religion because of its culture rather than its metaphysics.

Consider the 72% of people in England and Wales willing to declare their religion as Christian in the last census – a considerably higher proportion of the population than, according to other surveys, actually believes in a personal God. The content of their Christianity may be open to argument, but the figures suggest some sense of 'belonging' to a faith, irrespective of what they might believe, sufficient to make it a point of identification.

For the purposes of protective legislation, then, religious background can be reasonably added to the current recognition of 'colour, race, nationality or racial or ethnic origins'. There is no one criterion of identity around which a law can adequately be framed. Its scope depends on the particular social and cultural context, on which groups are understood to be vulnerable. If people are at risk of victimisation because of their religious heritage rather than their ethnic origin, then it makes sense to fine-tune the law.

As it happens, the prohibition of hate crime has a long precedent, going back as far as the Bible. One of the many commandments given to the Israelites in the wilderness was: 'You shall not abhor an Egyptian.'

■ Simon Rocker is a journalist with the *Jewish Chronicle*.
8 October 2005

© Guardian Newspapers Limited 2005

Group Name	Geographical Roots	Religion	Spoken	Written Regional/ National Language	Religious Language
Bangladeshis Bengalis	Sylhet region of Bangladesh, itself part of Bengal	Muslim (almost always, small percentage Hindu)	Bengali – often called Bangla; Sylheti dialect	Bengali	Classical Arabic
Indians (Panjabis)	Indian state of Panjab	Majority Sikh, some Hindus	Panjabi, many understand Hindi too	Panjabi for preference, Hindi for some	Panjabi Sanskrit for Hindus
Pakistanis	Pakistani state of Panjab	Muslim	Panjabi and Urdu (similar to spoken Hindi)	Urdu (uses different script from Hindi)	Classical Arabic
Indians (Gujeratis)	Indian state of Gujerat	Mostly Hindu, some Muslims	Gujerati, many speak Hindi too	Gujerati and Hindi	Sanskrit Classical Arabic for Muslims
Chinese	Hong Kong	Christian Confucian Buddhist	Cantonese Chinese, sometimes Hakka Chinese	Chinese (shares same characters as Mandarin Chinese)	No specific language
African-Caribbeans	British Caribbean Islands, e.g. Jamaica, Grenada, Trinidad	Christian, Rastafarian	English Creole of Patois (Patwa), or more likely a British form of it	Usually English	Rastas might use Patwa
Welsh	Wales	If any religion likely to be non-conformist Christian, e.g. Methodist	English and/or Welsh	Welsh and English	No specific language

NB: This chart tries to summarise a huge amount of complex information. While it has been carefully checked for mistakes, it over-simplifies some so it should only be taken as a guide.

Source: BritKid

Religiously motivated crime

Information from politics.co.uk

Faith 'hate crime' has risen nearly 600 per cent in London since the July 7th bombings, according to Scotland Yard.

The figures included verbal and physical attacks as well as criminal damage to property including mosques.

There were 273 incidents reported since the suicide bombings compared to only 41 over the same period (6 July to 1 August) year-on-year.

In the three days after the attacks, police recorded 68 faith hate crimes in the capital.

Scotland Yard said the increase was attributable to improvements in recording procedures and neighbourhood and borough-based policing.

Over the same period, racist and anti-Semitic incidents dropped, police noted.

The Islamic Human Rights Commission claimed last week the number of unreported attacks on Asians in Britain may have risen 13-fold since the London atrocities.

'Attacks were carried out right around the country in the aftermath of July 7th. The picture is by no means confined to London,' it said.

Inayat Banglawala, secretary of the Muslim Council of Britain, said attacks were carried out right around the country in the aftermath of July 7th.

'The picture is by no means confined to London,' he said.

3 August 2005

■ The above information is reprinted with kind permission from politics.co.uk. For more information, please visit www.politics.co.uk

© politics.co.uk

...ter the London bombings: sleepwalking to segregation

Britain is moving towards segregation, adding urgency to the need to drive forward the process of integration, the CRE announced today (22 September 2005) – information reprinted with permission from the Commission for Racial Equality

Speaking at Manchester Town Hall, Trevor Phillips, CRE Chair, said: 'Post 7/7 [the London bombings], the race relations industry has provided a vital post-emergency service which will have to be continued in the medium to long term to address the increasing segregation of our communities.

'The fact is that we are a society which, almost without noticing it, is becoming more divided by race and religion. We are becoming more unequal by ethnicity.

'If we allow this to continue, we could end up in 2048, a hundred years on from the *Windrush*, living in a Britain of passively co-existing ethnic and religious communities, eyeing each other uneasily over the fences of our differences.

'This is not only or even principally about Muslims. But the aftermath of 7/7 forces us to assess where we are. And here is where I think we are: we are sleepwalking our way to segrega-tion. We are becoming strangers to each other, and we are leaving communities to be marooned outside the mainstream.'

COMMISSION FOR RACIAL EQUALITY

Drawing on the recent example of New Orleans, Mr Phillips warned against complacency in the face of divisions and highlighted recent research by leading academics that gives a picture of 'hard' and 'soft' segregation in the UK:

- Increasingly, we live with our own kind. Residential isolation is increasing for many minority groups, especially South Asians: the number of people of Pakistani heritage in what are technically called 'ghetto' communities trebled between 1991 and 2001.
- New research from Bristol University shows that far from becoming sites of integration, children are slightly more segregated at school than in their neighbourhoods; and that means that neither children nor parents are mixing.
- Alongside this spatial segregation, there is also a trend towards 'soft' segregation, as different groups increasingly inhabit separate social and cultural worlds.
- New CRE research on people's friendship groups showed that for 95% of white Britons most or all of their friends are white. The proportion of ethnic minority Britons who have mainly or exclusively ethnic minority friends is 37%. These figures show

an increase from 94% and 31% respectively in the same study conducted last year.

Sources

1. Research: Findings of YouGov survey for the CRE (September 2005).
2. Press release: CRE survey shows little integration among UK's white majority community with ethnic minorities (19/07/04).
3. The trend is a cause for concern – younger Britons appear to be integrating less well than their parents.

Mr Phillips warned of the dangers of leaving this segregation unaddressed: 'When the hurricane hits – and it could be recession rather than a natural disaster, for example – those communities are set up for destruction. Even if there is no calamity, these marooned communities will steadily drift away from the rest of us, evolving their own lifestyles, playing by their own rules and increasingly regarding the codes that the rest of us take for granted as outdated behaviour that no longer applies to them.'

Integration agenda

Mr Phillips emphasised the importance of building an integrated society. He said: 'The fragmentation of our society by race and ethnicity is a catastrophe for all of us. We all have a part to play. Integration has to be a two-way street, in which the settled communities accept that new people will bring change with them and newcomers realise that they too will have to change if we are to move closer to an integrated society.

'We already know a lot about what an integrated society looks like. It has three essential features: equality, where everyone is treated equally, has a right to fair outcomes, and no one should expect privileges because of what they are; participation: all groups in society should expect to share in how we make decisions, but also expect to carry the responsibilities of making the society work; and interaction: noone should be trapped within their own community, and in the truly integrated society, who people work with, or the friendships they make, should not be constrained by race or ethnicity.

'There is no doubt that Britain is facing a clear demand to make the process of integration real, active and urgent.'

Mr Phillips also spoke of the critical need to encourage integration in education, both in schools and universities. He asked: 'Should we be considering using the funding system to encourage schools to attract a diverse range of children? Should we, the CRE, as part of our monitoring of local race equality schemes require them to show us that their catchment areas are being drawn in a way that encourages integration, rather than cutting them off from others who do not share their race? Ultimately, should we have a national understanding of what kind of mix is desirable and what undesirable?

'These are difficult questions, which will no doubt provoke cries of "social engineering". So be it. I would rather bear that albatross than allow our children to continue marching into educational ghettos.'

In order for people of different races and religions to mix, the CRE has already invested over £2 million in funding for sporting initiatives that help bring together Britain's diverse communities and has proposed the creation of summer camps for school leavers of all backgrounds.
22 September 2005

■ The above information is reprinted with kind permission from the Commission for Racial Equality. Visit www.cre.gov.uk for more or see page 41 for address details.
© *Commission for Racial Equality*

The reality of segregation

Trevor Phillips is not scaremongering . . . segregation is real and it's here in Britain!

Backing up Trevor Phillips' claims that Britain is becoming increasingly racially and religiously segregated, renowned academic Paul Gilroy says as the the comfort of multiculturalism ebbs away, communities' tendencies to self-protect thrives.

While many within the community are still discussing whether Trevor Phillips' claims that Britain is edging towards racial and religious segregation are really true or just a load of gibberish, renowned academic Paul Gilroy said the head of the Commission for Race Equality (CRE) is both 'right' and 'bold'.

In an interview with Black Britain the Professor of Social Theory at the London School of Economics (LSE) said although Britain didn't have 'legal [or] formal' segregation, 'I think

Trevor Phillips is right in pointing to the way that segregation is intensifying in the inner cities, interpersonal relationships and intensifying in the education system and I think those are real issues'.

'We are becoming strangers to each other'

In a speech last night (22 September 2005) made to Manchester council, Mr Phillips said that Britain was 'sleepwalking' its way into racial segregation and he also warned that some parts of the country were transforming into 'fully-fledged ghettos'.

Excerpts of Mr Phillips' speech were leaked to the press earlier this week in which he also said, 'We are becoming strangers to each other and leaving communities to be marooned.'

The comments came as the government announced that a year-long investigation into the alienation and prejudice experienced by black and ethnic people will be launched.

The emerging Commission for Integration and Cohesion will aim to build links with racial and religious groups often overlooked in political debate.

Professor Gilroy, who taught at the prestigious Yale University in the United States for 6 years, said the segregation is the 'effect' of many elements operating within the society, including how various communities throughout the country tend to stick together because of various reasons.

With events such as September 11, more recently the July 7 terror attacks in London and the Bradford race riots in 2001, the cracks in the well-polished British 'multicultural' façade are becoming more apparent and in some respects more destructive.

Poverty and inequality; the building blocks for segregation...

Professor Gilroy explained many people both inside and outside the black community are not necessarily as comfortable with the concept of multiculturalism that Britain once prided itself on because 'the idea of multiculturalism means that they are giving something up and they're having to not be themselves'.

He said many communities also tend to segregate themselves from mainstream society as an act of self-protection, safety and security in the face of hostility, suspicion and abuse.

Professor Gilroy added there are forms of segregation which people do 'to protect themselves and be themselves and there are forms of segregation that are there to do with the things that are done to them as they're victimised'.

With stringent government policies, such as stop-search and the recent war on terror, contributing to the intensification of segregation, particularly of certain 'religious groupings', Professor Gilroy said, 'If they are demonised as terrorists and criminals, they don't feel safe, so of course they are going to want to be with each other in small spaces.'

Referring to three of the London bombers, who came from particularly segregated and poverty-stricken areas around Leeds, he said:

'Where they're coming from, is maybe a more segregated kind of environment and maybe their interpretation of their experience and of the struggle in which they believed they were soldiers is fed by that experience of segregation somehow.'

With the financial divide playing an instrumental part in the construction of these 'ghettos', poverty and inequality are marginalising many within the black and poorer communities who have limited opportunities to help them get out of the 'ghettos'.

However, with the Commission on Integration and Cohesion aiming to search for ways 'to push further to tackle inequalities which can trap people into segregated lives', there are hopes the government will finally address the neglected issue of poverty, which affects so many within ethnic groups.

'When we talk about segregation we're looking at the effects of poverty and inequality that force people into certain areas,' Professor Gilroy said.

'Segregation becomes a problem within itself. It compounds the other kinds of racism that are there. It compounds the racism in the education system and the inequality that is there in the housing system and the job market and the labour market are all compounded by segregation.'

Education can close the door on segregation...

Agreeing that education is the 'fundamental dynamic', Professor Gilroy said by giving people the same opportunitities, creating less segregation and creating a British identity all can relate to, then 'the educational institutions have a very special role to play and they need to be worked on'.

Mr Phillips also called for integration within the education system and for it to be more representative of British society, minimalise inequality and increase the likelihood of smashing the poverty cycle.

Calling for 'creative' solutions rather than positive discrimination to target increasingly ethnic-segregated schools and promote diversity, he told the BBC some universities are now becoming 'colour-coded' and that more ethnic minority students should be accepted.

Sylvia Watts-Cherry, the Director of the Education Advance Services Ltd, nonetheless, said to make schools and universities take on ethnic minority students is not necessarily going to shepherd educational institutions towards integration and diminish segregation.

'I think it's hard to make people that don't want to, take children just because they are black – I'm not sure if that's the way,' she told Black Britain.

'Those people who are accepted have to be accepted because they're good and they're not being accepted just because they're black.'

Having gone to a Scottish school where she and her siblings were the only black pupils, Ms Watts-Cherry said to put ethnic minority students in an environment where they cannot relate to anyone and where they are not wanted, for the sake of integration, can have long-term detrimental effects.

She recalled: 'It was very hard growing up around with nobody else that understood how I felt and finding out that teachers in private underestimated me was very, very difficult.

'If certain religious groupings are demonised as terrorists and criminals, they don't feel safe, so of course they are going to want to be with each other in small spaces'

'On the face of it they told me that they expected me to do well and later found out some basically didn't expect me to do anything at all and that broke my heart and to this day it still affects me.'
Scharene Pryce
23 September 2005

■ Printed with permission of Black Britain (www.blackbritain.co.uk), part of the Colourful Network. For more information see page 41.
© The Colourful Network

Why Trevor is wrong about race ghettos

Equality chief Trevor Phillips was wrong when he claimed our cities are divided by racial groups, says population expert Prof Danny Dorling. The real threat is the growing divide between rich and poor

'Ghettos in English cities almost equal to Chicago' ran a headline last week. 'Sleepwalking to segregation' began an editorial in *The Times*.

All this resulted from a speech made in Manchester by the chairman of the Commission for Racial Equality, Trevor Phillips, last Thursday (22 September 2005). He had some interesting points, but his central claim – that we are drifting toward racial segregation – is wrong.

> ## Racism is rife in Britain but it is not being expressed through rising levels of neighbourhood segregation, nor are any ghettos likely to be formed in the near future

Racial segregation is not increasing, as he claimed. There are no neighbourhood ghetto communities in Britain, and the 'new' research he cited to try to support his claims is neither new nor authoritative.

The carefully considered conclusion of academics in Britain is that there are no ghettos here. In short, Phillips has been ill informed, or has simply not understood what his organisation has been telling him. Racism is rife in Britain but it is not being expressed through rising levels of neighbourhood segregation, nor are any ghettos likely to be formed in the near future.

If ignorance of these trends extends as far as the chairman of the CRE, the debate on segregation in Britain will be the poorer for it, and we will neglect the segregation that really is occurring: by poverty and wealth.

Had Phillips read the work of the academic who has studied segregation in most detail in Britain over recent years he might have thought more carefully. In fact if he had only read the first two sentences of Dr Ludi Simpson's most recent paper he would have learnt that 'racial self-segregation and increased racial segregation are myths for Britain. The repetition of these myths sends unhelpful messages to policy makers.'

The most up-to-date segregation statistics for ethnic and religious groups were published more than a year ago. They were calculated from the latest census and are comparable with figures a decade earlier. For all ethnic minority groups identified by the census, the indices of segregation fell between 1991 and 2001. These are the indices to which Phillips referred in his speech. They fell fastest for people of black and 'other Asian' origin.

For no ethnic minority group have these indices risen. In contrast, segregation rose over the same period in Northern Ireland for many religious groups. The pattern in particular cities will vary slightly, but nationally ethnic minority neighbourhood segregation in Britain is falling – and there are no ghettos, no neighbourhoods where a single ethnic minority group is in the majority. This has happened in America, where they are called minority-majority areas.

Even if there were such areas in Britain there is no reason to see that as a problem, but before proposing opinions, it is important to get the facts right.

What may have confused Phillips is work reported by an Australian-based academic at a conference last summer which referred to the extent to which different groups in Britain may be becoming more isolated rather than more segregated. It is not hard to see why the indices academics use to measure these things could so

easily be confusing. The segregation index is a measure of the proportion of people who would have to move home for a group to be evenly spread across the country. It is falling for all minorities.

By contrast, the index is a measure of how often individuals from a particular group are likely to meet other individuals from their group. Communities suffer high levels of isolation if most of them live together with few other ethnic groups. Low levels of isolation come in communities where ethnic minority groups are more spread out and where other groups live in relatively high numbers.

The two are related but do not measure the same thing. Most crucially, if disproportionate numbers of people in a particular group are of child-bearing age and have children, raising the size of the group, the index of segregation remains the same, while the so-called index of isolation rises. That is a simple function of population growth among younger communities, of whatever ethnic origin. It does not reveal very much about levels of isolation.

The index of isolation is thus not necessarily a good measure to use, but if the CRE chairman does refer to it, it might be useful for him to

know that it is highest in Britain for Christians, followed by people with no religion.

The most segregated religious groups in England and Wales are people of the Jewish and Sikh faiths, not Muslims as is often supposed; while the levels of geographical isolation of people of Catholic faith in Scotland exceed those of any minority religious or ethnic group in England. All these facts are taken from a couple of pages of the *2001 Census Atlas of the UK*. That was published in 2004 but there are now many other sources of this data to show that no neighbourhood ghettos are being formed in Britain.

Our schools and universities are becoming more unequal in their intake, but not necessarily by religion nor by ethnicity

---

There are shocking statistics concerning segregation that Phillips does need to address. In some areas African-Caribbean boys are up to 15 times more likely to be excluded from school than are white boys, and up to 12 times more likely to be incarcerated in prison in Britain. Children and young people are being segregated out of classrooms and disproportionately into prisons by ethnicity in this country. The CRE has enough real work to do that it does not need to create fictitious evils.

In terms of education Phillips is right to say that children are more segregated by school than by neighbourhood, but this is only slightly so and it has only once been measured – so he was wrong to imply that schools are increasing the trend towards racial segregation. Our schools and universities are becoming more unequal in their intake, but not necessarily by religion nor by ethnicity.

What is most unfortunate is that this misunderstanding detracts from the neighbourhood segregation that is most clearly occurring in Britain

but which is about poverty and wealth, not race nor religion. Neighbourhoods are becoming more segregated by rates of illness and premature mortality. Depending on when and to whom a baby is born, inequalities in their chances of reaching their first birthday have widened since 1997. Neighbourhoods are rapidly becoming more segregated by wealth – most clearly by housing equity through which the best-off tenth of children should each expect to inherit £80,000 simply because of where they were born.

The racial ghettos referred to in Phillips' speech do not exist. However, had his researchers looked at the census more carefully then they would begin to see much else that should concern them. Cut Britain up horizontally rather than by neighbourhood, and you do find minority-majority areas. For example above the fifth floor of all housing in England and Wales a minority of children are white. Most children growing up in the tower blocks of London and Birmingham – the majority of children 'living in the sky' in Britain – are black.

Phillips needs the census to tell him what is happening as much as any of the rest of us do. Our gut feelings are not good enough, our own lives too isolated for us to extrapolate from experience.

The evidence comes mainly from social statistics. Increasingly, Britain is segregated by inequality, poverty, wealth and opportunity, not by race and area. The only racial ghettos in Britain are those in the sky in neighbourhoods which are, at ground level, among the most racially mixed in Britain, but where the children of the poorest are most often black.

We have not been sleepwalking into segregation by race, but towards ever greater segregation by wealth and poverty. That matters most to the life chances of people in Britain.

■ Danny Dorling is professor of human geography at the University of Sheffield and co-author of *People and Places: A 2001 Census Atlas of the UK*, published by the Policy Press. This article first appeared in the *Observer*, 25 September 2005.

© *Guardian Newspapers Limited* 2005

Challenging multiculturalism

Teacher who challenged multiculturalism had to sacrifice his job

By Tom Leonard

The discovery that the four London bombers were British Muslims has ensured that one of the great social debates of the next few years will be on the sensitive issues of racial ghettos, integration in schools and multiculturalism.

Fear of being labelled racist has helped to ensure that few have dared to put their heads above the parapet and challenge the orthodoxy that Britain is a multicultural nation and must behave like one. Ray Honeyford, a Bradford headmaster, was one of the first and most significant critics to challenge publicly multiculturalism's central tenet that all cultures in Britain are equally valid and no single tradition should be dominant.

As the head of Drummond Middle School in Bradford, where 90 per cent of pupils were Asian, Mr Honeyford was concerned about the consequences of encouraging children to cling to their own ethnic group rather than integrate.

> **Multiculturalism's central tenet is that all cultures in Britain are equally valid and no single tradition should be dominant**

In a series of articles published in the right-wing *Salisbury Review* in the early 1980s, he criticised Bradford city council's policy of educating ethnic minority children according to their own culture, predicting that the move would create divisions between white and Asian communities.

At school, where languages such as Urdu, Gujurati and Hindi predominated over English, Mr Honeyford tried to introduce a uniform but he was opposed by the local council, which judged that such a move could be racist. Concerned that 'we were getting nine-year-olds who had never sat in the same class as a white child', Mr Honeyford wanted to impose racial integration – if need be, by busing in white pupils from across the city.

His views provoked an outcry among the anti-racism lobby. Some picketed the school and Mr Honeyford was subjected to personal abuse and accused of racial prejudice – leading to his early retirement in December 1985 to save his family from further harassment. He wrote later that he was told he had been forced out because his attitudes were 'racist' and his insistence on integrating Asian children was 'dangerous and damaging'.

RAY HONEYFORD

Although Mr Honeyford remained a pariah for the education establishment, ironically, many of his views were later echoed by Herman Ouseley, one of the country's leading anti-racism campaigners. Lord Ouseley was a former head of the Commission for Racial Equality, which had been one of Mr Honeyford's main critics.

In his report about race relations in Bradford following rioting by Asian and white youths in 2001, Lord Ouseley blamed fear, ignorance and segregation in the city's schools for preventing integration and tolerance.

His report concluded that self-segregation was driven by exclusively Asian or white schools, and ignorance of each other's religions and communities. The main problem within the schools had to be addressed by citizenship classes, he added.

Community leaders were upset by the report and accused the peer of failing to understand the city's 'complexities'.

A year later, Lord Ouseley complained that his recommendations had been largely ignored and blamed Bradford's leaders for failing to act. Mr Honeyford, meanwhile, claimed that the report justified what he had been saying years before. However, Estelle Morris, the Education Secretary at the time, later acknowledged that ministers needed to do 'some serious thinking' in the wake of the report.

In an attempt to stem mounting opposition to an expansion of faith schools, she revealed plans to impose new rules to ensure that they were 'inclusive' by taking children from other faiths or forming partnerships with non-religious schools by sharing teachers or arranging joint activities.
14 July 2005
© *Telegraph Group Limited 2005*

Muslims 'take pride' in British way of life

Britons endorse multi-cultural society – as British Muslims say immigrants should 'integrate fully'

Most British Muslims support British laws and culture, and do not believe Islam is incompatible with British democracy, according to new research from MORI.

The survey, for the BBC, shows the views of British Muslims are largely in line with other members of the British public. In fact, in some areas Muslims more strongly advocate integration than non-Muslims. They are more likely than British people to demand that Muslim clerics preach in English, for example, and that immigrants be made to learn English.

Ben Page, Director of the MORI Social Research Institute, said: 'This survey shows, quite clearly, that there is far more that unites the British people than divides them. Only a minority feel that Islam is incompatible with British culture, and most British Muslims feel immigrants should be made to integrate fully into British society.

'When it comes to British sporting achievement, for instance, Muslims are as likely to say they feel proud of international success as other members of the British public.'

The survey shows that 62% of British people – and 82% of Muslims in Britain – agree with the statement: 'Multiculturalism makes Britain a better place to live'. When asked if the policy of multiculturalism is a mistake that should be abandoned, 68% of people (74% Muslims) disagreed.

When asked if they felt proud by British sport teams doing well in international events, 90% of Britons (88% Muslims) say they do.

On the topic of immigrants coming to Britain, 82% (90% Muslims) say they should be made to learn English, 73% (76% Muslims)

say they should pledge their primary loyalty to Britain, 73% (69% Muslims) say they should integrate fully into British society and 96% (95% Muslims) say they should accept the rights of woman as equal citizens.

'There is far more that unites the British people than divides them'

Half of British people (49%) and two-thirds of British Muslims (66%) do not think that Islam is incompatible with the values of British democracy.

Significant differences appear, however, on issues related to the Government's response to the threat of international terrorism – 60% of British Muslims say it is unacceptable to detain suspected terrorists without trial, compared to 36% of the public. Almost three-quarters of British Muslims (72%) say it is unacceptable to stop and search people on the

basis of their race, compared with two-thirds (65%) of the public.
10 August 2005

Technical details

MORI interviewed a nationally representative sample of 1,004 GB adults aged 16+ by telephone. Data are weighted to reflect the population profile. In addition, 204 booster interviews were conducted among Muslims. 112 interviews were conducted with Muslims who had agreed to be recontacted in previous representative surveys. The remaining 92 interviews were conducted using Random Digit Dialling in 27 local authority areas in groups of wards with over 10% Muslim residents according to the UK census. These data are weighted to reflect the overall Muslim population profile. All interviews were conducted on 8-9 August 2005.

■ Information from MORI. Please visit www.mori.com for more information.

© MORI

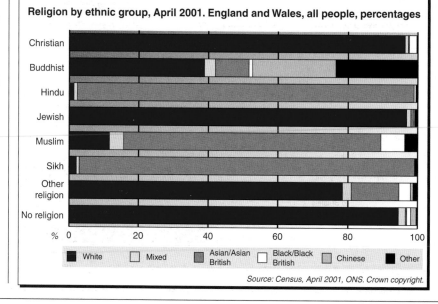

Religion by ethnicity

Religion by ethnic group, April 2001. England and Wales, all people, percentages

Source: Census, April 2001, ONS. Crown copyright.

British identity

YouGov/*Daily Telegraph* survey results: YouGov questioned 3,05 adults aged 18+ throughout Britain online between 20th and 22nd July 2005, asking them to indicate how important they felt each word or phrase below was in defining Britishness '. The results have been weighted to the profile of all adults.

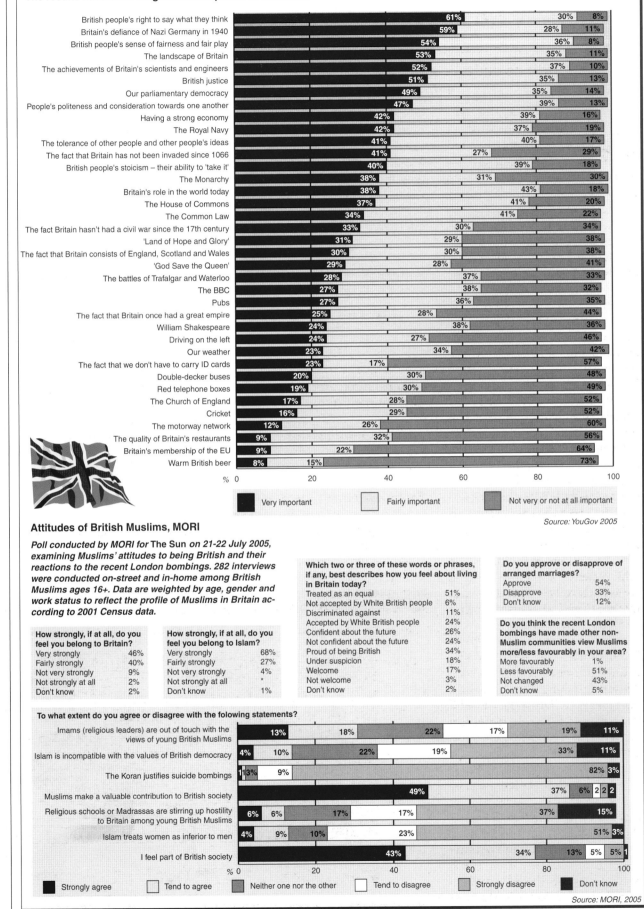

Source: YouGov 2005

Attitudes of British Muslims, MORI

Poll conducted by MORI for The Sun *on 21-22 July 2005, examining Muslims' attitudes to being British and their reactions to the recent London bombings. 282 interviews were conducted on-street and in-home among British Muslims ages 16+. Data are weighted by age, gender and work status to reflect the profile of Muslims in Britain according to 2001 Census data.*

How strongly, if at all, do you feel you belong to Britain?	
Very strongly	46%
Fairly strongly	40%
Not very strongly	9%
Not strongly at all	2%
Don't know	2%

How strongly, if at all, do you feel you belong to Islam?	
Very strongly	68%
Fairly strongly	27%
Not very strongly	4%
Not strongly at all	*
Don't know	1%

Which two or three of these words or phrases, if any, best describes how you feel about living in Britain today?	
Treated as an equal	51%
Not accepted by White British people	6%
Discriminated against	11%
Accepted by White British people	24%
Confident about the future	26%
Not confident about the future	24%
Proud of being British	34%
Under suspicion	18%
Welcome	17%
Not welcome	3%
Don't know	2%

Do you approve or disapprove of arranged marriages?	
Approve	54%
Disapprove	33%
Don't know	12%

Do you think the recent London bombings have made other non-Muslim communities view Muslims more/less favourably in your area?	
More favourably	1%
Less favourably	51%
Not changed	43%
Don't know	5%

To what extent do you agree or disagree with the folowing statements?

Imams (religious leaders) are out of touch with the views of young British Muslims — 13% | 18% | 22% | 17% | 19% | 11%

Islam is incompatible with the values of British democracy — 4% | 10% | 22% | 19% | 33% | 11%

The Koran justifies suicide bombings — 1% 3% | 9% | 82% | 3%

Muslims make a valuable contribution to British society — 49% | 37% | 6% | 2 | 2

Religious schools or Madrassas are stirring up hostility to Britain among young British Muslims — 6% | 6% | 17% | 17% | 37% | 15%

Islam treats women as inferior to men — 4% | 9% | 10% | 23% | 51% | 3%

I feel part of British society — 43% | 34% | 13% | 5% | 5% | 1

Strongly agree · Tend to agree · Neither one nor the other · Tend to disagree · Strongly disagree · Don't know

Source: MORI, 2005

Two-thirds of Muslims consider leaving UK

By Vikram Dodd

Hundreds of thousands of Muslims have thought about leaving Britain after the London bombings, according to a new *Guardian*/ICM poll.

The figure illustrates how widespread fears are of an anti-Muslim backlash following the July 7 bombings which were carried out by British-born suicide bombers.

The poll also shows that tens of thousands of Muslims have suffered from increased Islamophobia, with one in five saying they or a family member have faced abuse or hostility since the attacks.

Police have recorded more than 1,200 suspected Islamophobic incidents across the country ranging from verbal abuse to one murder in the past three weeks. The poll suggests the headline figure is a large underestimate.

The poll came as British Islamic leaders and police met to try to boost recruitment of Muslim officers, improve efforts to protect Muslims from a backlash, and improve the flow of information from Muslims to the police about suspected terrorist activity.

Nearly two-thirds of Muslims told pollsters that they had thought about their future in Britain after the attacks, with 63% saying they had considered whether they wanted to remain in the UK. Older Muslims were more uneasy about their future, with 67% of those 35 or over having contemplated their future home country compared to 61% among those 34 or under.

Britain's Muslim population is estimated at 1.6 million, with 1.1 million over 18, meaning more than half a million may have considered the possibility of leaving.

Three in 10 are pessimistic about their children's future in Britain, while 56% said they were optimistic.

Nearly eight in 10 Muslims believe Britain's participation in invading Iraq was a factor leading to the bombings, compared to nearly two-thirds of all Britons surveyed for the *Guardian* earlier this month. Tony Blair has repeatedly denied such a link.

Muslim clerics' and leaders' failure to root out extremists is a factor behind the attacks identified by 57% of Muslims, compared to 68% of all Britons, and nearly two-thirds of Muslims identify racist and Islamophobic behaviour as a cause compared to 57% of all Britons.

The general population and Muslims apportion virtually the same amount of blame to the bombers and their handlers, with eight in 10 or more citing these as factors.

The poll finds a huge rejection of violence by Muslims with nine in 10 believing it has no place in a political struggle. Nearly nine out of 10 said they should help the police tackle extremists in the Islamic communities in Britain.

Tens of thousands of Muslims have suffered from increased Islamophobia, with one in five saying they or a family member have faced abuse or hostility since the London bombings

A small rump, potentially running into thousands, told ICM of their support for the attacks on July 7 which killed 56 and left hundreds wounded – and 5% said that more attacks would be justified. Those findings are troubling for those urgently trying to assess the pool of potential suicide bombers.

One in five polled said Muslim communities had integrated with society too much already, while 40% said more was needed and a third said the level was about right.

More than half wanted foreign Muslim clerics barred or thrown out of Britain, but a very sizeable minority, 38%, opposed that.

Half of Muslims thought that they needed to do more to prevent extremists infiltrating their community.

■ ICM interviewed a random sample of 1,005 adults aged 18+ by telephone on 15-17 July 2005. Interviews were conducted across the country and the results have been weighted to the profile of all adults. ICM is a member of the British Polling Council and abides by its rules. Further information at www.icmresearch.co.uk

26 July 2005

© *Guardian Newspapers Limited 2005*

Proud to be British?

Education, jobs and transport key to Asian Britishness

First-generation Asians in Britain are less likely to view themselves as 'British' if they are unemployed, cannot speak English or do not have access to decent public transport according to the Institute for Public Policy Research (ippr).

A working paper published today (Tuesday 2 March 2005) – based on interviews with Asian people in Tameside, Greater Manchester – shows that only a small number of interviewees said that they did not feel 'British' at all. The working paper recommends that government conduct an annual review to monitor the integration of ethnic minorities more effectively. It argues that this should focus on levels of educational achievement and employment rates.

Danny Sriskandarajah, ippr Senior Research Fellow, said:

'The better we understand what life has been like for migrants, the better we can explain how they feel toward their adopted country. We cannot expect all migrants to feel British overnight, but this research assures us that an overwhelming majority of the British Asians interviewed do have a sense of belonging in Britain. The key is to make sure that they are welcomed properly, don't feel discriminated against and are given the skills they need to contribute to society effectively.'

Dr Andrew Thompson, author of the working paper, said:

'In recent years, the Government has put plenty of effort into improving levels of educational achievement and rates of employment among migrants. We are arguing for a more rigorous assessment of what is being done, focusing on outcomes rather than target setting. Central government should ensure that integration is not impeded by factors that lie within its control. The more impediments to integration can be removed, the more established migrant communities and new-

comers are likely to demonstrate a sense of belonging to British society, and to espouse the "core British values" that the CRE, the Community Cohesion Panel and others hope to see.'

The survey indicates that social isolation is worse among Asian, mainly Muslim, women but help is needed to integrate all of Britain's Asian communities, not just British Muslims. Despite recognising the importance of practical support given to ethnic minorities by their own schools, shops, places of worship and community centres there is a need to ensure that housing and education policy does not create mono-cultural neighbourhoods. Interaction in the workplace is identified as an important factor to learning English and encouraging social integration, as is an increase in mobility through access to affordable public transport.

The survey was conducted in Tameside, Greater Manchester. An equal number of men and women were interviewed. Ages ranged between 49 and 86. The majority of interviewees were in their sixties or early seventies, the average age being 68. Interviewees arrived in Britain between 1956 and 1979 from India, Pakistan, Bangladesh, Kenya and Uganda. Asian people represent about 4 per cent of the population of England and Wales, and 4.6 per cent of the population of Tameside.

Notes

- *Asian 'Britishness': A study of first generation Asian migrants in Greater Manchester* is written by Dr Andrew Thompson, Pro-Dean for Learning & Teaching in the Arts Faculty, and Senior Lecturer in Modern History, at the University of Leeds, with Rumana Begum, who worked in the Race Equality and Diversity Unit of Tameside Council.
- ippr's Asylum and Migration Working Paper Series has been established to provide a vehicle for examining the evidence in relation to specific aspects of policy and practice in this area.
- Information on case studies is available from the ippr press office.

2 March 2005

■ The above information is reprinted with kind permission from the Institute for Public Policy Research. Visit www.ippr.org.uk for more information.

© IPPR

Identity

9 in 10 of Mixed group identify as British

National identity

In most non-White ethnic groups in Britain, the majority of people described their national identity as either British, English, Scottish or Welsh. This included 88 per cent of people from the Mixed group, around 80 per cent of Pakistanis, Black Caribbeans and Bangladeshis, and three-quarters of the Indian and Other Black groups.

76% of Bangladeshis said they were British, while only 5% said they were English, Scottish or Welsh

---

People from the White British group were more likely to describe their national identity as English (58 per cent) rather than British (36 per cent). However, the opposite was true of the non-White groups, who were far more likely to identify themselves as British. For example, three-quarters (76 per cent) of Bangladeshis said they were British, while only 5 per cent said they were English, Scottish or Welsh.

Country of birth

Among people living in Great Britain, the proportion born in the UK (England, Wales, Scotland or Northern Ireland) varied markedly by ethnic group.

Other than the White British group, those most likely to be born in the UK were people from the Mixed ethnic group and from the Other Black group, 79 per cent in each. This reflects their younger age structure. A substantial proportion of the Other Black group were young people, who were born in Britain, and who chose to describe their ethnicity as Other Black and wrote in 'Black British' as their answer. Black Caribbeans were the next most likely group to be born in the UK.

Among the non-White ethnic groups the proportions born in the UK generally declined with age. For example, 83 per cent of Black Caribbeans aged 25 to 34 were born in the UK, but this fell sharply with age so that only 5 per cent of those aged 45 to 64 were born in the UK. For some other non-White ethnic groups (Black Africans, Chinese and Bangladeshis) this sharp decline occurred in younger age groups, reflecting their later immigration.

Sources

- Annual local area Labour Force Survey 2002/03, Office for National Statistics;
- Census, April 2001, Office for National Statistics;
- Census, April 2001, General Register Office for Scotland.

Published on 21 March 2005

- Information from the Office for National Statistics.

© Crown copyright

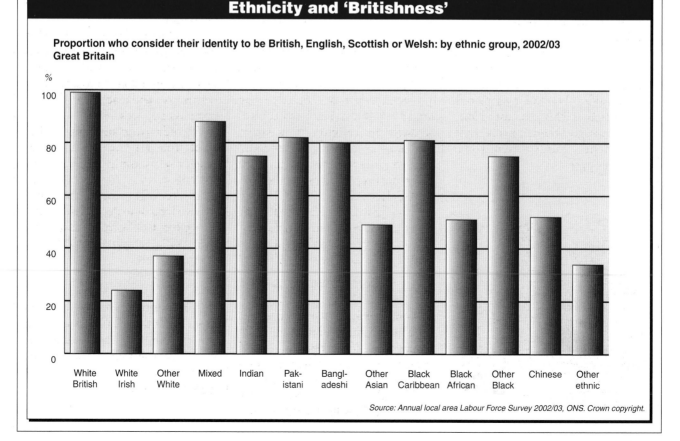

Ethnicity and 'Britishness'

Proportion who consider their identity to be British, English, Scottish or Welsh: by ethnic group, 2002/03 Great Britain

Source: Annual local area Labour Force Survey 2002/03, ONS. Crown copyright.

Mixed-faith relationships

Most relationships require compromise and effort if they are going to succeed, but what about when you come from different religious backgrounds?

When I started seeing my boyfriend, the reaction from my friends and family was mixed. Some were none too impressed and some told me it would have no chance of working. I was even asked why I didn't go out with someone 'normal'. So what was wrong with my boyfriend? He's a Muslim... and I'm not.

Muslim men? They're all Bin Laden-worshipping fanatics who don't allow their four wives to work, aren't they? Those are just some of the stereotypes I've had to deal with. Admittedly, Britain is becoming increasingly tolerant of mixed-religion relationships, but in many cases you'll find that some of the old taboos and prejudices still remain.

Degrees of difference

Whatever background you come from, there will always be some differences between you and your partner, but they won't necessarily be based on your religious beliefs. However, if you completely disagree on important issues you may find life difficult.

Put things into perspective. You don't always have to agree with your partner, in fact it can make life interesting to be close to someone who disagrees with you, just as long as those disagreements don't become monumental hurdles that you'll never get over.

Negative reaction

Friends might believe stereotypes about a religion and have negative reactions to your choice of partner at first. Explain to them how you feel about your partner and let them meet each other and form their own opinions based on the person rather than the religion.

Family business

Both your family and your partner's family may have problems accepting the relationship. Your partner may choose to keep your existence a secret from them. It doesn't feel nice to be someone's dirty secret but you have to try to be understanding.

21-year-old Ali, a Muslim, had a three-year relationship with a Catholic girl. He chose to keep the relationship a secret from his family. 'Girlfriends aren't allowed in Islam,' he explains. 'My family would be ashamed and my Dad would probably have disowned me. Keeping the relationship secret was an emotional drain and made my girlfriend feel uncomfortable, but I didn't feel like I had a choice.'

According to relationship adviser Matt from askTheSite, this kind of problem isn't uncommon. 'The main problem people face when getting into a relationship with someone of a different religion is negative reactions from family and friends,' he says. So what can you do? 'The most important factors are respect and understanding – for your family and your partner. Be prepared to sit down and discuss issues; listen as well as talk. You need to address problems without steaming in with demands.'

Cultural differences

You may have to get used to certain customs, such as removing shoes, special diets and celebrating religious holidays. Keep an open mind and remember it doesn't hurt to compromise. 'Sometimes I felt my girlfriend was insensitive to my culture and I disliked that,' says Ali.

Make an effort to learn about your partner's religion so you understand their point of view. Some things may seem strange at first, but if you stay together long term, they will quickly seem natural. If you are unwilling to make small changes it's unlikely that the relationship will work in the long run.

Happily ever after...

However, when it comes to bigger issues such as moving in together, marrying and having children, it's important to talk early on and set some boundaries on how much you're willing to change. If either of you have strong feelings that your children should be brought up in a certain way, for example, you will need to come to some agreement about it.

Sarah, 22, was in a three-year relationship with a Hindu man. 'I'd never go out with someone of a different religion again after my bad experience,' she says. 'I think it's easier being with someone the same as yourself.'

Ali disagrees. He thinks there is a lot to be gained from mixed-religion relationships. 'Being with someone of a different religion broadens your perspective and teaches you how to compromise,' he says.

According to relationships adviser Matt from askTheSite, a mixed-religion relationship can be a success so long as the couple work at it. 'Whether the relationship will survive long term depends upon the strength of feeling involved and the two people putting the effort in to making it work.'
By Katy Muench

■ The above information is reprinted with kind permission from TheSite.org. For more information on this issue as well as many others, please visit their website at <u>www.thesite.org</u>

© TheSite.org

■ Racism is treating someone differently or unfairly simply because they belong to a different race or culture. People can also experience prejudice because of their religion or nationality. (page 1)

■ The majority of the UK population in 2001 were White (92%). The remaining 4.6 million (or 7.9%) people belonged to other ethnic groups. (page 3)

■ The word racism comes from this word. 'Race' was used by scientists in the 19th century to classify groups of people by the colour of their skin. Scientists have now proved that all of us, as human beings – black, white or brown – have the same ancestors. (page 4)

■ People often use the term 'ethnic minority' when they mean Black and Asian people, though ethnic has nothing to do with colour. The Irish in Britain are a minority ethnic group. (page 5)

■ The Race Relations Act is concerned with people's actions and the effects of their actions, not their opinions or beliefs. Racial discrimination is not the same as racial prejudice. (page 7)

■ In the last year for which statistics are available, 2003-04, there were 52,694 racist incidents recorded, a seven per cent rise from 49,078 in the previous year. (page 9)

■ The number of children charged with race crimes in Scotland has soared by 74 per cent in the past three years. (page 9)

■ Only 23% of large companies in the UK have equality procedures in place and in small companies the situation is even worse – 97.5% have no equality practices in place at all. (page 13)

■ Nearly two-fifths (39 per cent) of Pakistani employees and nearly half (47 per cent) of Bangladeshi employees have never been offered training. (page 14)

■ In 2004, 17 per cent of the maintained school population in England was classified as belonging to a minority ethnic group. (page 18)

■ Teaching black boys separately could help them learn more quickly, according to a leading black American academic. (page 21)

■ Britain has the highest level of mixed-race relationships in the developed world. According to the 2001 Census of England and Wales, there were 219,000 marriages between people from different ethnic backgrounds. (page 24)

■ Inter-ethnic marriages account for only 2% of all marriages in England and Wales. (page 25)

■ Members of a faith group are born into a community, rather than a set of doctrines. Some may feel their religious identity to be more a matter of family ties than theological conviction. (page 26)

■ Bangladeshis or Bengalis in the UK are almost always members of the Islamic faith, although a small percentage are Hindu. (page 27)

■ Faith 'hate crime' has risen nearly 600 per cent in London since the July 7th bombings. (page 27)

■ The number of people of Pakistani heritage in what are technically called 'ghetto' communities trebled between 1991 and 2001. (page 28)

■ New research from Bristol University shows that far from becoming sites of integration, children are slightly more segregated at school than in their neighbourhoods; and that means that neither children nor parents are mixing. (page 28)

■ Most British Muslims support British laws and culture, and do not believe Islam is incompatible with British democracy, according to new MORI research. (page 34)

■ In a poll by YouGov, 'British people's right to say what they think' was identified as the most important feature of 'Britishness' by respondents. (page 35)

■ 43% of British Muslims surveyed by MORI strongly agreed with the statement 'I feel part of British society', while 34% tended to agree. (page 35)

■ Tens of thousands of Muslims have suffered from increased Islamophobia since the London bombings, with one in five saying they or a family member have faced abuse or hostility since the attacks. (page 36)

■ First-generation Asians in Britain are less likely to view themselves as 'British' if they are unemployed, cannot speak English or do not have access to decent public transport according to the Institute for Public Policy Research (ippr). (page 37)

■ In most non-White ethnic groups in Britain, the majority of people described their national identity as either British, English, Scottish or Welsh. This included 88 per cent of people from the Mixed group, around 80 per cent of Pakistanis, Black Caribbeans and Bangladeshis, and three-quarters of the Indian and Other Black groups. (page 38)

You might like to contact the following organisations for further information. Due to the increasing cost of postage, many organisations cannot respond to enquiries unless they receive a stamped, addressed envelope.

Black History Month
Well Placed Consultancy
106 Baker Street
LONDON
W1M 8TW
Tel: 0207 642 9728
Email: info@black-history-month.co.uk
Website: www.black-history-month.co.uk
This site will celebrate Black History Month all year round. We will regularly update it and use it to educate, inform, and build confidence. Let's celebrate and share our African and Caribbean history.
Black History Month (BHM) is held every October in Britain. The aims are to:
■ Promote knowledge of Black History and experience
■ Disseminate information on positive Black contributions to British society
■ Heighten the confidence and awareness of Black people in their cultural heritage.

BritKid
University College Chichester
College Lane
CHICHESTER
West Sussex
PO19 6PE
Tel: 01243 816000
Website: www.britkid.org

ChildLine
45 Folgate Street
LONDON
E1 6GL
Tel: 020 7650 3200
Fax: 020 7650 3201
Email: reception@childline.org.uk
Website: www.childline.org.uk
Children can call ChildLine on 0800 1111 (all calls are free of charge, 24 hours a day, 365 days a year).
ChildLine is the UK's free helpline for children and young people in danger or distress. Provides confidential phone counselling service for any child with any problem 24 hours a day. Produces publications. Children or young people can phone or write free of charge about problems of any kind to: ChildLine, Freepost 1111, London N1 6BR, Tel: Freephone 0800 1111. Children who are deaf or find using a regular phone difficult can call ChildLine's textphone service on 0800 400 222.

The Colourful Network
3rd Floor, Culvert House
Culvert Road
LONDON
SW11 5AP
Tel: 08700 76 5656
Fax: 08700 76 5757
Email: info@thecolourful.net
Website: www.blackbritain.co.uk
Black Britain was launched in July 1998 to deliver immediate and regular news and information services to the Black and ethnic minority communities, and to address the shortcomings of mainstream media.

Commission for Racial Equality
St Dunstan's House
201-211 Borough High Street
LONDON
SE1 1GZ
Tel: 020 7939 0000
Fax: 020 7931 0429
Email: info@cre.gov.uk
Website: www.cre.gov.uk
The Commission for Racial Equality is working for racial equality for a just society, which gives everyone an equal chance to work, learn and live free from discrimination and prejudice, and from a fear of racial harassment and violence. Produces a wide range of factsheets, books and other resources. Ask for their publications list.

Kick It Out
Unit 3
1-4 Christina Street
LONDON
EC2A 4PA
Tel: 020 7684 4884
Fax: 020 7684 4885
Email: info@kickitout.org
Websites: www.kickitout.org
www.farenet.org
Kick It Out was established as an independent organisation with funding from the Professional Footballers' Association (FPA), the Football Association (FA), the Football Trust and the FA Premier League. The group took up the role of furthering the objectives of highlighting and campaigning against racism in football at all levels.

The 1990 Trust
Room 12, Winchester House
9 Cranmer Road
LONDON
SW9 6EJ
Tel: 020 7582 1990
Fax: 0870 127 7657
Email: blink1990@blink.org.uk
Website: www.blink.org.uk
Black Information Link (BLINK) is the main communication channel of the 1990 Trust. Its vision is the elimination of racial discrimination, the realisation of human rights for all.

Trades Union Congress (TUC)
Congress House
23-28 Great Russell Street
LONDON
WC1B 3LS
Tel: 020 7636 4030
Fax: 020 7636 0632
Website: www.tuc.org.uk
The TUC is the voice of Britain at work. With 70 affiliated unions representing nearly seven million working people from all walks of life, we campaign for a fair deal at work and for social justice at home and abroad. We negotiate in Europe, and at home build links with political parties, business, local communities and wider society.

INDEX

ACKNOWLEDGEMENTS

The publisher is grateful for permission to reproduce the following material.

While every care has been taken to trace and acknowledge copyright, the publisher tenders its apology for any accidental infringement or where copyright has proved untraceable. The publisher would be pleased to come to a suitable arrangement in any such case with the rightful owner.

Chapter One: Race Issues

Racism, © ChildLine, *Population size*, © Crown copyright is reprinted with the permission of Her Majesty's Stationery Office, *Words*, © BritKid, *Racism – what is it?*, © Kick It Out, *Word rage*, © The Voice, *What is racial discrimination?*, © Commission for Racial Equality, *What is racial harassment?*, © The Monitoring Group, *Police log over 1,000 racist incidents a week*, © Telegraph Group Ltd 2005, *Schools under fire as child race crimes rocket 74%*, © The Scotsman, *Victims of crime*, © Crown copyright is reprinted with the permission of Her Majesty's Stationery Office, *Racism at work*, © TUC, *Discrimination in employment*, © Black Britain, *Racism in the workplace*, © TUC, *Black History Month*, © Black History Month, *Black history and education*, © Black Britain, *Ethnicity and education*, © Crown copyright is reprinted with the permission of Her Majesty's Stationery Office, *Why black kids fail at school*, © Black Information Link, *Boosting Black achievement*, © Crown copyright is reprinted with the permission of Her Majesty's Stationery Office, *Black boys 'do better in a class of their own'*, © 2005 Associated Newspapers Ltd, *Breaking stereotypes*, ©

Commission for Racial Equality, *Mixed blessings*, © Guardian Newspapers Ltd 2005, *In the mix*, © Guardian Newspapers Ltd 2005.

Chapter Two: Race, Faith and Identity

Face to faith, © Guardian Newspapers Ltd 2005, *Main British language and religious groups*, © BritKid, *Religiously motivated crime*, © Monitoring Group, *After the London bombings: sleepwalking to segregation*, © Commission for Racial Equality, *The reality of segregation*, © Black Britain, *Why Trevor is wrong about race ghettos*, © Guardian Newspapers Ltd 2005, *Challenging multiculturalism*, © Telegraph Group Ltd 2005, *Muslims 'take pride' in British way of life*, © MORI, *Two-thirds of Musims consider leaving UK*, © Guardian Newspapers Ltd 2005, *Proud to be British?*, © IPPR, *Identity*, © Crown copyright is reprinted with the permission of Her Majesty's Stationery Office, *Mixed-faith relationships*, © TheSite.org.

Photographs and illustrations:

Pages 1, 21, 30, 36: Simon Kneebone; pages 6, 24, 33: Angelo Madrid; pages 7, 18: Bev Aisbett; pages 12, 23, 31, 37: Don Hatcher; pages 14, 32: Pumpkin House.

Craig Donnellan
Cambridge
January, 2006